BETTER DAILY
MINDFULNESS HABITS

BETTER DAILY MINDFULNESS HABITS

Simple Changes with Lifelong Impact

KRISTEN MANIERI

ROCKRIDGE
PRESS

Series Designer: Angela Navarra
Interior and Cover Designer: Patricia Fabricant
Art Producer: Sara Feinstein
Production Editor: Mia Moran
Production Manager: Jose Olivera

Author photo courtesy of Arlene Laboy

ISBN: Print 978-1-64876-981-8 | eBook 978-1-64876-982-5

R0

To Marc, Elizabeth, and Aly . . .
home is wherever you are.

CONTENTS

INTRODUCTION

My friend Angie is a smart, conscientious, and kind person. She meditates and journals most days, regularly processes her feelings with select friends, and generally places personal growth as a high priority in her life. And yet her ability to move through the world with more awareness, lightness, and love can sometimes fall short. At times, she finds herself feeling triggered, annoyed, and stuck. It's as though she misplaces her mindful self. When she regains it, Angie is left feeling discouraged and disappointed with herself. It's easy to relate to Angie's predicament. Mindfulness is easy; the hard part is remembering to be mindful.

Anyone can cultivate the skill of mindfulness. You've likely experienced a time when your attention suddenly becomes focused on something right in the moment, regardless of how fleeting. The concept of present-moment awareness isn't complex. But to live steeped in such awareness is another story. It's not as easy to continuously orient the mind to the present.

The reason that staying focused on the present is challenging is because the brain is designed for mindlessness *and* mindfulness, and both forces are at work simultaneously and continuously. There are the mindless parts of the brain that look to automate our consistent behaviors so that a larger portion of our existence can be put on cruise control, thus conserving energy for other neuronal pursuits. Activities like brushing your teeth, starting your coffeemaker, and even resting your head on your pillow each night are automated behaviors that likely occur completely outside your consciousness. And then there are the mindful parts of the brain that delight in the now, like when you savor a sunset and become besotted by a baby's coo. At times like these, it's easy to drop deeply into a moment, with full consciousness, and be profoundly moved.

Both parts of the brain are important and beneficial, but the automated mind, or the one that produces mindlessness for the purpose of survival and efficiency, often has far too many slices of the pie. But here's the good news: you can learn to turn the tables and give the mindful mind more of its fair share. In fact, you can leverage the power of the automated mind to create habits and rituals that flood your life with presence, compassion, and insight.

Several years ago, I began establishing a daily practice of meditation. Rising early in the morning, I sat on my cushion to meditate. When my practice was finished, I felt immensely calm, centered, and clearheaded. But then life would happen. It's inevitable ups and downs and twists and turns would disrupt my sense of calm and throw me off track. Although I could sense that my practice often kept me steady, resilient, and present, I would too often lose my center and mental clarity.

A daily meditation practice, no matter how solid or consistent, won't eliminate the automated mind, which will always switch back on. However, when you integrate the science of habits with the art of daily mindfulness, you will discover a formula for an awakened life.

PART 1

HABITS AND MINDFULNESS

The capacity to be present and aware is a gift embedded in our human design. Every person has the ability to contemplate experiences and even think about thinking.

Scientists have found that through self-directed neuroplasticity, metacognition, and intrapersonal attunement, it is possible to redirect the mind and change your level of awareness.

A reliable tool for making these changes is habit. Any activity you do with enough consistency becomes automated and no longer requires deliberate focus. In effect, it becomes effortless. Using the power of habits, mindfulness can become effortless, too.

Whether your goal is to become more present and productive or compassionate and creative, the first step is turning your awareness to the present moment. Mindfulness habits, coupled with the right intention and attention, etch grooves in the brain that allow you to return to your awareness over and over again.

What Is Mindfulness?

I t's rare to be present in the now. Steeped in thoughts of yesterday, five minutes from now, or next week, it's all too easy to miss the moment you're in. And yet the present moment is where life is lived and savored.

In a way, a life without mindfulness is not living. It's just thoughts about living. But when you deliberately drop into the present and bring your awareness to this meal, this conversation, this yoga pose, this 10-year-old child's hand in yours, this embrace, this scent of magnolia in the air, this ray of sun on your skin, this sip of tea, then you are living.

What Does It Mean to Be Mindful?

According to the Greater Good Science Center at UC Berkeley, mindfulness means "maintaining a moment-by-moment awareness of our thoughts, feelings, bodily sensations, and surrounding environment, through a gentle, nurturing lens." This definition points to how to become cognizant of what's happening around you and, perhaps more important, what's happening inside you.

You bring a special kind of awareness to your experiences: an awareness seasoned with curiosity, kindness, openness, and acceptance. It's as though you are a researcher collecting data about your life as you live it. Your approach is inquisitive, compassionate, and non-judgmental, aimed at understanding instead of fixing, progressing not perfecting.

In this way, mindfulness is a flashlight that illuminates your experience. It's a tool that helps you see more clearly, savor more deeply, and live more wisely. It's the portal through which you reconnect with yourself and see who you truly are underneath the societal conditioning. If you choose, it's the doorway into a deeper understanding of your inner world and the world around you.

Regardless of the words used to define it, mindfulness matters. Why? Because each of us only gets this one life, and none of us gets to know how long it will last. It matters that you are able to fully experience and appreciate it.

Barriers to Mindfulness

You can set up an incredible support system of habits to cultivate mindfulness and conscious living, but it's all for nothing if you don't also take the time to remove the hurdles that impede your ability to be mindful.

There are a number of behaviors that may seem to calm or steady you in times of stress or that can give a false sense of accomplishment in your daily life. In the long run, these behaviors can sabotage your mindfulness goals.

Technology: Smartphones have become a seemingly indispensable part of daily life. The trouble is, smartphones and apps distract you from the present moment and entice you into unconscious, repetitive behaviors, like scrolling mindlessly dozens of times each day.

Lack of self-care: The better you care for yourself, the better you become at responding to life's inevitable challenges and trials. Sleep, good nutrition, regular meals, rest, exercise, play, and connection with others are just some of the many elements that help you fill your resilience tank and live with more presence.

Multitasking: Most of us have developed the skill of being able to do many things at once. No wonder mindfulness is a challenge. No matter how clever you are at stacking multiple tasks, each task will suffer from the lack of your full attention. It's truly impossible to connect with others, yourself, and the present moment when you are doing several things at once. Part of the intention to live a more mindful, conscious life is the commitment to doing only one thing at a time.

Clutter: Besides creating a sense of sanctuary, simplicity, and cleanness, an organized environment can help you feel more grounded and freer from distraction. Clutter can make you feel hemmed in to the point that you feel robbed of your energy and gusto. But when you begin to eliminate your external chaos, you simultaneously settle your inner seas.

Lack of solitude: Solitude, when it's chosen, is beneficial. The time you spend on your own gives you space to contemplate your life and to discover who you are. It is in the gaps between your interactions with others that you power down and access your intuition, creativity, and insight.

Why Be Mindful?

Now that you understand what mindfulness is, what it is not, and what can get in the way of mindfulness, it's time to dig into the reasons that being mindful is beneficial. You may feel that present-moment awareness is all well and good, but perhaps what you really want is to be:

MORE COMPASSIONATE-------- > LESS JUDGMENTAL

MORE PATIENT-------------------- > LESS HURRIED

MORE EASYGOING--------------- > LESS RIGID

MORE CALM----------------------- > LESS ANXIOUS

MORE PRESENT------------------ > LESS DISTRACTED

MORE DISCIPLINED------------- > LESS ERRATIC

MORE SELF-LOVING------------- > LESS SELF-CRITICIZING

MORE GENEROUS---------------- > LESS SELFISH

MORE GRATEFUL ----------------- > LESS ENTITLED
MORE JOYFUL --------------------- > LESS MOODY
MORE CONSCIOUS -------------- > LESS ASLEEP

Although presence is a central tenet of mindfulness, on a deeper level, it's about who you are when you consciously direct and choose how you want to show up in the world. Consciously being true to who you are in the present can improve your life on many levels.

On one level, mindfulness can influence your relationships. A true sense of safety and belonging comes from how well you are able to form healthy and solid attachments to yourself and to the people in your life. According to an eight-decade-long study outlined in the book *The Longevity Project*, harmonious relationships are a key indicator of health and may impact health and longevity even more than diet and genes. By practicing mindfulness, you can access the presence of mind needed to make your relationships better and, as a bonus, improve your health and happiness.

Mindfulness also creates white space, gaps in between activity, and stillness or silence amid internal chatter and external noise. Mindfulness allows you time to pause, even if only for a second or two, so you can return to yourself.

Do you sit with your thoughts and feelings, especially difficult ones, long enough to let them pass? Or do you need to distract yourself as quickly as possible? Mindfulness helps you better withstand discomfort, not so you can become a titan of pain but to enable you to let the pain pass.

Beyond Meditation

Meditation is a highly effective tool for training the brain to be more mindful, but it's not the only tool. As you'll see in the pages ahead, there are many practices you can use to cultivate more presence and focus every day.

For example, although the breath is often used as a point of focus in meditation, you can access it anytime throughout the day to reorient yourself to the present moment. A few mindful breaths can induce a similar experience of calm and ease as sitting on your meditation cushion for 20 minutes.

When you breathe in, you activate the sympathetic nervous system, which engages your "go" mode. If your sympathetic nervous system is engaged, such as when you are in a fight-or-flight response, you'll find yourself breathing in more and taking in more oxygen, which can help you deal with the stressor you are facing.

But on the opposite side of that seesaw is the para-sympathetic nervous system, which activates your "slow" mode. A long, slow exhale engages the parasympathetic nervous system. Deliberately slowing down the breath sends signals to the body and brain that you are safe and solid.

By slowing down and bringing your full attention to your actions, you are, in essence, turning that action into a moving meditation. When you look beyond the meditation cushion, you find all sorts of places to integrate mindfulness into your life.

I like to think of my morning meditation as the rudder of my day; it's what begins to steer me in the direction

I want to go. But then I must keep steering. My daily mindfulness practice helps keep my hands on the wheel.

Bringing Mindfulness into Your Life

It's a beautiful thing to bring mindfulness to your daily activities, such as washing hands, walking, hugging, and eating. In fact, the more mobile and portable you can make your mindfulness habits, the more integrated they become in the everyday living of your life. Moreover, most of us have far more time for informal mindfulness practices than we do for formal meditation, so it makes sense to make informal practice your top priority. Begin to think of all of your daily activities as entranceways to conscious living.

Truly, every moment is an invitation to cultivate your ability to be in the now. This was a concept I first discovered when I read Eckhart Tolle's book *The Power of Now* over a decade ago. I learned that thinking and consciousness are not the same thing and that when I free myself from my ceaseless inner dialogue, there is a space of stillness and wakefulness where a treasure trove of opportunities to expand, grow, and savor are buried.

This book is designed to weave mindfulness into your life, which I hope is especially heartening if you have struggled to find the time or patience for a formal meditation practice. While I don't discount the value of daily meditation, it's not the only doorway to mindfulness. Whether your goal is to become happier, be less stressed, or simply feel more satisfied in your life, the habits ahead will support your goals without the need to set aside extra time each morning for formal meditation.

A Mindfulness Mindset

Throughout this book, you will find mindfulness practices that have been strategically designed to become habits in your everyday life. Using the power of the automated mind, mindfulness will begin to take less and less effort. But one word of caution: you don't want to become so automated in your mindfulness habits that you begin to do them on autopilot. This is why it's important to weave a particular mindset into this endeavor.

Jon Kabat-Zinn, founder of the internationally renowned Mindfulness-Based Stress Reduction (MBSR) program, often shares that the path to a mindful life requires intention, attention, and attitude.

→ Set an **intention** to use these practices to cultivate awareness of the present moment.
→ Deliberately bring your **attention** and focus to what is happening right now.
→ Nurture an **attitude** of nonjudgment, patience, curiosity, and kindness toward yourself and your practice.

As I've heard a few mindfulness teachers say, practicing without all three—intention, attention, and attitude—is like rowing a boat that's still tied to the dock.

KEY TAKEAWAYS

- A mindful life is one in which you're present enough to truly feel and experience what's happening in each moment. Without it, you're sleepwalking through your days and missing out on the essence of living.
- Mindfulness means having an awareness of the present moment, both inside and around you, in a curious and nonjudgmental way.
- Mindfulness is about being present, but it's really about who you are *being* in the present. When you have more awareness, you increase your capacity to be more kind, thoughtful, compassionate, loving, and wise.
- You can create a more mindful life by removing the barriers that make mindfulness difficult, such as technology, lack of self-care, multitasking, clutter, and a lack of solitude.
- While meditation is an effective tool for cultivating more mindfulness, there are many practices you can weave into everyday living that make learning to be mindful less effortful.
- By cultivating a mindful intention, attention, and attitude, you bring a mindset to your habits that helps keep you present and aware.

CHAPTER 2

How Habits Can Build Mindfulness

Daily life is erected on an invisible foundation of habits. Whether you're aware of it or not, you're always building habits, and your days are filled with them. And yet habits aren't accidental; they're a strategic element of our human architecture, and they're built in a highly predictable and steadfast way.

Consciously focusing on habit-building and leveraging the habit loop to create positive behavioral changes is what this book is all about. As you'll learn, you can use the power of the automatic mind to live with more awareness, presence, and peace.

Habits 101

A habit is any behavior that is repeated routinely. The more ingrained a habit, the more you are likely to do it without conscious focus or intent. In a sense, habits are behaviors that are done effortlessly and mindlessly.

Chances are your life is already filled with many behaviors you no longer consciously decide to do. I don't decide each morning to brush my teeth; I just do it because it's a habit I started decades ago. If you take a quick inventory of your day, you're likely to discover that a large part of it is made up of behaviors that are done routinely.

Habits serve an incredibly important function. Each day, your body has a finite amount of energy to devote to keeping you alive. These resources need to be strategically and efficiently allocated in real time. When a behavior is habituated, it no longer requires the same level of brainpower as it did when you first performed it, which frees up energy for more important priorities like threat assessment, innovation, and problem-solving.

Because the brain is constantly seeking to convert repeated behaviors into habits so it can manage energy more efficiently, it will create a habit even when that's not your intention. This is especially true of bad habits. Often, upon reflection, bad habits seem like they just happened.

Your health, happiness, career, finances, and relationships are defined to a much lesser degree by behaviors that you engage in once in a while than by the things you do over and over again. Lasting behavior change depends on the ability to turn the healthy behavior you want to do into a behavior that you do *without* having to use willpower and motivation as the fuel. When you create healthy habits, automation becomes the fuel.

The Habit Loop

When it comes to modifying behaviors or adopting new behaviors, most people tend to rely far too heavily on motivation and willpower, believing that desire and discipline alone should bring their goals to fruition. But motivation and willpower are fickle friends, and they're not always able to support you when the going gets tough.

In its simplest form, habit-building occurs inside a cue-routine-reward loop, also called a habit loop. An internal or external trigger, or cue, provides the brain with a prompt to carry out a specific behavior, or routine. The routine produces a reward, which provides an incentive for the brain to repeat the loop the next time it experiences the cue. Over time, the brain converts a conscious behavior into an unconscious routine that requires less intent, effort, or focus. For example, my 6 a.m. alarm triggers my morning meditation habit, which helps me feel grounded and centered during the day. Finishing my dinner triggers my ice cream habit, which rewards me with delicious flavors and a sugar bump. Seeing my phone triggers my checking text messages habit, which makes me feel like I'm "caught up" with friends and colleagues.

BJ Fogg, a Stanford behavior scientist and author of *Tiny Habits*, offers another way to look at behavior change using prompts, or cues. Fogg sees habits as being anchored in our lives. He explains that by stacking new behaviors with existing habits, you can better integrate new habits into your life.

Using his *Tiny Habits* formula, Fogg helps people thoughtfully design and troubleshoot behaviors they would like to become habits. It goes like this: *After I* _____ , *I will* _____. For example, my formula for practicing my ukulele looks like this: *After I put on my pajamas, I will practice my ukulele for five minutes.*

Fogg also suggests that after you complete the behavior you're hoping to habituate, you immediately give yourself a feel-good reward by having a little celebration. Even a quick "woo-hoo" or an internal high five has the power to orient the mind toward a behavior again and again simply because it felt good. Rewarded behaviors are repeated behaviors.

What's Happening in the Brain

Without the capacity to turn recurring activities into habits, everyday living would take an enormous amount of time, focus, and effort. We'd all be exhausted by lunchtime. Luckily, repeating specific skills and activities allows the brain to turn them into habits, freeing up energy for other important functions and focused pursuits.

The trouble is, the brain is extremely good at automating our behavior–almost too good. Around 90 percent of the brain's activity is subconscious. Things like beliefs, values, biases, and bodily functions exist in a default state. But since these defaults impact so much of the brain's activity, choices, and behaviors, they are enormously powerful. To make any real and lasting behavior changes, the changes need to happen at the level of our unconscious, or automatic, mind, which is where habits live.

Lucky for us, the brain has neuroplasticity, which mean it is malleable and changeable. In other words, parts of the brain can be deliberately strengthened, just as you would strengthen a muscle in your arm or leg. Self-directed neuroplasticity is a process that explores how to strategically and intentionally rewire your own brain.

Habits are a key ally in this rewiring process. In essence, by using the brain's innate habit-building tendency, you're adopting new behaviors that better serve you and reinforcing them by creating strong neural connections through repetition and continued use.

What about Bad Habits?

The habit-building process has no moral compass; it doesn't care whether a habit is "good" or "bad" for us. The brain identifies a repeated behavior, and regardless of whether that behavior makes us sick or successful, it forms it into a habit. As a result, we're just as likely to form bad habits as we are good habits. In fact, since so many of our bad habits have pleasing rewards associated with them, bad habits tend to be stickier.

A bad habit is any behavioral pattern with a negative or harmful result. Obvious things, like smoking or gambling, may come to mind. But the truth is that most of us have at least a few seemingly innocuous unhealthy habits. In my own life, I can see procrastinating, slouching, and nail-biting as just a few bad habits I've developed over the years. When observed over a single day, these might seem harmless, but when observed daily over a lifetime, it's easier to see how these habits have a huge cumulative effect.

According to Leo Babauta, who authors the popular site Zen Habits, bad habits can be caused by the desire to alleviate boredom or stress. Whether it's an unhealthy habit of needing a few glasses of wine to "take the edge off" the day or mindlessly scrolling through social media feeds in between appointments, it's hard to justify the value of these repeated actions.

Besides eroding your health, bad habits can negatively impact your sense of self, and a positive self-image is essential in order to make healthy changes and become the person you want to be. Without a positive self-image, it is much easier to become discouraged and self-defeating.

Conversely, as you begin to develop good habits and witness the results, your belief that you can rely on yourself grows, becoming a source of encouragement and self-confidence. This confidence, along with self-compassion, is crucial to successfully implementing change and achieving your goals.

Breaking Bad Habits

One of the most effective ways to break a bad habit is to replace it with a better one. Since the habit loop is already formed and etched in the brain, simply trying to stop the negative behavior with willpower can be very difficult. Willpower is often no match for a long-standing habit, no matter how great the desire for change.

Instead of using willpower, a finite resource, it's more effective to wield the power of habits, which requires much less energy and conscious effort. In essence, what you're doing is suffocating the bad behavior with a new good habit. For example, I replaced the habit of looking at my phone in waiting rooms with the habit of reading a book while I wait.

You can also break bad habits by adding friction, as Wendy Wood explains in her book *Good Habits, Bad Habits: The Science of Making Positive Changes That Stick*. By adding restraining forces, such as making a habit harder to do by removing triggers and changing your environment, you modify the context for your habit, which gives it less fuel. On the opposite end of the scale, you can support your good habits by making them easier to do and cultivating environments where they can thrive.

Let's look at stress reduction, for example. If you currently release or manage stress with a few unhealthy habits, instead of eliminating those behaviors, replace them with healthier habits. This benefits you in two ways. First, you upgrade the habit loop with a behavior that supports you. Second, as you experience less stress, you become more adept at meeting your craving and temptation with more awareness and discernment. Mindfulness habits, in particular, strengthen your sense of equanimity so you no longer need dopamine hits from harmful habits in order to feel calm and steady. You can use your own inner guidance system to reduce stress rather than looking outside yourself for a remedy.

Mindfulness Habits

As you begin to adopt some of the mindfulness habits in the pages ahead and start to eliminate and replace bad habits, you'll find that your capacity for healthy habit-building grows. That's because mindfulness habits not only serve you in the moment—by helping you feel calmer and more present—but also begin to rewire the brain for more awareness overall. When you're more aware, you are less likely to succumb to unconscious bad habits because you're simply paying more attention. You start to know yourself better and see your patterns and tendencies more clearly; then you begin to live more mindfully more often.

You'll find that mindfulness habits are a little different than other habits, and that's because they require a special type of mindset. As you learned in chapter 1, intention, attention, and attitude are essential to the cultivation of mindfulness habits. In other words, how and why you do something are as important as what you are doing. For example, if you choose to pause for three mindful breaths as you begin a meal, you're not simply going through the motions of breathing three times before you reach for the fork. Instead, you have an intention to be present and sincere. You deliberately turn your attention to the breath and bring an attitude of patience and curiosity to the moment. Your reward is a greater potential for calm and presence.

Your mindset has incredible influence over how you experience your life. To mold and direct your mindset with deliberateness means that you choose and navigate not only what you think about but how you think about it. It's an astonishing and indispensable tool on the mindful path.

Finally, it's been helpful for me to relate to mindfulness as a place I visit rather than a permanent state I'm trying to achieve. In that vein, think of the habits in this book as doorways or portals to awareness. Each time you use one, you will be visiting a still and wise place inside yourself. The more you practice, the longer you will visit.

Bad Habit Loops

Bad habit loops can crop up almost without you noticing. Just like good habits, some of those bad habit loops may take root quickly, some may take more time to establish, and some will fail to launch. How firmly established a habit loop becomes depends on how it is built and rewarded. In order to avoid bad habit loops and practice good habit hygiene, you will need to be self-aware, thoughtful, and deliberate. The ability to avoid bad habit loops and the ability to nurture good habit loops go hand in hand. Here are some ways you can do both.

Monitor progress: Monitoring your habits will help you create positive change, which is why you'll find a habit tracker at the end of each chapter in part 2. Keeping track of your progress gives you a realistic overview of what you have done, but more important, it will provide you with insights about bad habits that are particularly sticky and good habits that are struggling to take root so you can make any necessary adjustments.

Provide friction for bad habits: Make your bad habits hard and your good habits easy. Have whatever tools you need ready to go. Share your plans with people in your life so you're not having to explain yourself in the moment. Make bad habits inconvenient, look ahead to predict future obstacles for habits you are establishing, and then solve them before they ever happen. Be your bad habit's nemesis and your good habit's best ally.

Get back on track: When you fall off your good habit, it's a common mistake to put off restarting it until Monday or until the first of the month. Delaying will only cause you to lose precious momentum and put you in a bad habit loop of procrastination. If you miss a day or veer off the trail, commit to getting back on track immediately.

Celebrate: Amp up the feel-good vibes in your good-habit-building process by immediately celebrating yourself each time you do your new good habit, especially if that good habit is replacing a bad habit. While it might feel silly, your brain will wire more deeply around feel-good behaviors. Don't be afraid to give yourself a cheer for every little win.

Small Changes, Big Results

Most behavior stems from unconscious habits, and most habits are built unconsciously. Imagine the power of consciously-built habits that not only steep your life in a greater sense of calm, composure, and resilience but also help you live with more awareness. This is the power of mindfulness habits and the reason even the smallest of habits have an enormous impact.

Small changes practiced with consistency yield big results over time. Each new habit represents a baby step, and each step begins to rewire the brain. Accomplishing your goals in quantum leaps is tempting, but when you're building new habits, the proverb holds true–slow and steady wins the race.

As you begin to move through the habits offered in the pages ahead, a word of caution: you may not build them all, and you especially won't build them all at once. In fact, you'll want to be focused on just a few at a time.

Habit-building is a task best performed method-ically and systematically. If you launch too many cue-routine-reward sequences at once, your attempts to establish them all as steadfast habits will fall short. I sug-gest focusing on establishing no more than four habits in a single month, though this book offers you space to track the beneficial and unhelpful habits that are discussed in each chapter, if you so desire.

When it comes to habit-building, the brain needs single-mindedness, and the more you can narrow your effort and focus on a specific task, the more attuned your mind becomes to it. Soon the brain realizes that it's using a lot of energy to place so much emphasis on this one repetitive task, and it begins to move the task into its unconscious processes. Once your unconscious pro-cesses kick in–boom!–you're on your way to creating a healthy new habit.

Start small and scale carefully. If you are adding a new sequence and you recognize that a previously established habit is starting to erode, drop the new sequence and return your focus to the one that needs reinforcement. This "presence project" is a process, not an event. Rome wasn't built in a day. Your mindful life won't be, either.

KEY TAKEAWAYS

- Most behaviors stem from habits, which are created through the cue-routine-reward habit loop.
- The brain is designed to turn repeated behaviors into habits in order to free up energy for other tasks.
- Bad habits are formed the same way good habits are. The trouble is, bad habits often have pleasing rewards, which make them especially sticky and hard to break.
- You can break bad habits by slowly replacing unhealthy behaviors with beneficial ones.
- New habits need to be built methodically and systematically. Take baby steps to slowly build up momentum rather than shooting for big changes in short periods of time, as dramatic changes will likely prove unsustainable.

PART 2

HOW TO BUILD MINDFULNESS HABITS

Habits are built methodically using the cue-routine-reward loop. As you troubleshoot and learn how to make habits stick, you'll expand your ability to cultivate consistent behaviors. Because these are mindfulness habits, you'll also expand your ability to notice how these new behaviors impact your life and how they make you feel and think differently.

We are always works in progress. The time that we take to self-reflect, to know ourselves more deeply, and to harness the power of our own insight is a lifelong project that's not about perfecting but rather understanding ourselves. By building habits that give us access to our mindful selves, we connect to an inner guidance system, looking inward instead of outward for wisdom, steadiness, and direction.

Approach your mindfulness journey like a scientist who is curiously observing, inquiring, and collecting data. Practicing is the journey, and there is no destination.

CHAPTER 3

Being Present in Your Body

Wherever you go in life, whatever you do, one thing is for sure: your body will be there with you. So, it makes sense that on your journey to cultivate mindfulness, you begin with habits that support being more present in your body. Much like a mother attunes to her baby's needs, you can orient your attention inward to discover what nourishment or nurturing your body might be quietly asking for. Through the process of becoming self-attuned, you will learn to become your own greatest ally.

Mindful Body

Your body houses a tremendously helpful alert system for navigating your needs, thoughts, and emotions. Something as simple as a 60-second check-in can provide boundless intel about your inner world. When you close your eyes, you may sense that you're thirsty, a little tight in your midback from being at your computer all day, or frustrated from a conversation you had earlier in the morning. What was lurking below now floats to the surface to be tended.

Being present in the body is a homecoming, a rein-habiting, an opportunity to return to and re-engage with yourself. It's where you can quite literally come to your senses, or what Jon Kabat-Zinn calls "falling awake." Attuning to the present moment, most often through the senses, allows you to experience the delight and beauty of being alive.

Of course, you may encounter physical or emotional pain as you look inward, which can make tuning in to the body uncomfortable. But through mindfulness, you can begin to cultivate a friendliness, or at least a sense of solidarity, toward what's happening inside, even if you don't like it. As you turn toward yourself and create habits of tending to and accepting your body—its shape, sensations, and stages—you turn resistance, struggle, and aversion into acceptance, compassion, and love.

You are experiencing life with and through your body. The habits ahead will support you as you create a mindful body connection.

Building Healthier Habits

I've noticed that the people around me who are thriving tend to take really good care of themselves. It can take a lot of effort to get through the day, but those people who have maintained deliberate habits of self-care seem to have boundless energy and vibrancy.

When you fill up your tank and refuse to run on fumes, you begin to tap into endless resources that not only give you what you need to do your work but also keep you steady when the unpredictable winds of adversity inevitably blow your way.

There are five mindful body practices in this chapter, all designed to turn your awareness inside the body. Healthy habits that attune you to your inner world provide the gateway to better self-care and a sense of harmony with yourself. Mind-body connection isn't just a spiritual pursuit; it's a pragmatic practice. Imagine driving a car without a dashboard. You'd never know your speed, gas level, tire pressure, or oil level. Thankfully, your car has gauges for all of these key metrics, which allows you to care for your car and keep it running. You, too, have a dashboard. The habits that follow will help you see it and respond to it.

Stop and Drop

During my Mindfulness-Based Stress Reduction (MBSR) training, I learned to use the acronym STOP as an effective way to quickly drop into the body. STOP stands for Stop, Take a breath, Observe, and Proceed. Think of it like tapping your brakes when you're moving full speed ahead. When you learn to connect to the body for just 30 seconds, you can slow down long enough to notice what's happening inside and around you, raising your awareness of your environment, thoughts, emotions, and physical sensations.

Start by gently closing your eyes or relaxing your gaze as you place one hand or both hands on the middle of your chest. Bring your attention to one inhale and one exhale, without any intention to change or deepen the breath. Just be with this one in-and-out breath. Internally, say "hello" to your body and this moment; then look to label your experiences on the inside and outside with single words. Perhaps the words "busy," "stressed," "tight," or "tired" come to mind. Maybe you notice you're thirsty, hungry, or clenched. Tend to your needs; take a sip of water, grab a snack, or gently roll your shoulders and neck.

An ideal cue for this habit is specific transitions. Use any time you shift from one task to another, move from one place to another, or come and go from your home as a prompt for this stop and drop practice. Your reward is having more energy because you have attended to your body's needs. Aim to practice this habit several times a day.

Do a Mindful Body Scan

Scanning the body for emotions, tension, and discomfort is a useful way to quickly tune in to your physical state and triage your needs. It's also a way to detect and diffuse stress. The body has a physiological response to the fast-paced, overly demanding world, which is to flood the body with hormones such as cortisol. By tuning in to your stress response, you can begin to release it.

Start in a seated position. Close your eyes and take a few grounding breaths. Repeat an anchoring phrase in your mind, such as "I am here now." Beginning with your feet, slowly bring your awareness to the body's sensations. As your awareness travels up through the body, notice any warmth, tension, or even absence of sensation. If your mind wanders, which it will, repeat your anchor phrase, breathe, and bring your attention back to where you left off. When you reach the top of your head, finish by taking a few deep breaths, and perhaps even place your hand on your heart as a sign of friendly camaraderie with yourself.

Connect this practice to a cue you experience frequently, such as waiting. This could include waiting for your kettle to boil or a Zoom call to start. Notice moments when you'd normally "kill time" by checking your phone, and choose instead to do a quick three- to five-minute body scan. You will benefit by feeling more grounded and more connected to your body.

Take 10 Steps

When I first learned this walking meditation, I found that it took an agonizing amount of effort. As I followed my teacher's instructions to slowly and deliberately place one foot in front of the other, being careful to notice each and every sensation, I experienced a gnawing urge to speed up and walk at my regular pace. Walking meditation felt so awkwardly sluggish. But as my resistance slowly faded, I discovered how lovely it was to carefully attune my steps to the world around me. Eventually it became surprisingly pleasurable to bring so much attention to something I do so mindlessly every day.

As you stand to begin, take a moment to feel centered and present. Notice your tendency to rush toward your destination rather than being aware of the journey. At a pace that feels comfortable to you (perhaps half your usual speed), begin taking one mindful step, noticing the sensations in the foot, knee, and leg as you are in motion. Repeat for nine more steps, keeping your attention locked on each movement. After 10 steps, return to your regular pace and take note of any internal shifts that may have occurred.

To turn taking 10 mindful steps into a habit, anchor it to arrivals. Whether you're stepping out of your car to walk into the grocery store, meeting up with a friend, or returning home, turn the first 10 steps into a walking meditation. Park as far away from your destination as possible so you can truly enjoy the process. Your focused presence in this process will bring you a sense of vitality and will help your body feel alert and alive.

Wash Your Hands

Handwashing is a necessary task that is usually performed several times a day. Of course, it prevents the spread of germs, but it also allows a 30-second opportunity to come home to yourself and reinhabit the body. The small act of mindfully cleaning your hands is a way to connect to your intention to have a loving and warm relationship with yourself.

As you turn on the tap, take a moment to feel centered and present. You may choose to close your eyes or softly place your gaze on your hands. First, take a mindful breath and tune in to the sound of the water. Bring your hands under the tap and notice the physical sensation of water on your skin. After you've added soap, tune in to this new physical sensation as well as any scent you experience from the soap. Almost as if in slow motion, softly wash the fronts and backs of the hands and fingers and in between the fingers. Take this time to drop deeply into the experience and tune in to any thoughts, emotions, or sensations in your inner world.

As you begin to implant the habit of mindfully washing your hands and using this action to reconnect to yourself, it may be helpful to place a sticky note on the bathroom mirror for the first week as a cue to wash mindfully. This brief, simple habit rewards you by providing comfort, good health, and an increased connection to the self.

Take Three Mindful Breaths

Breathing is an essential part of living and well-being, yet most breaths pass without any reverence, attention, or intention whatsoever. That's a shame considering the crucial role breath plays for not only surviving but thriving. The breath helps regulate your inner equanimity, it influences your nervous system, and it serves as a red flag for unease. Tight, constricted, shallow breathing shines a spotlight on anxious, fretful, and uneasy thoughts and emotions.

Place one or both hands on the middle of your chest and gently close your eyes. Starting with an inhale, follow the breath with your focused attention as it passes through the nostrils, down the throat, into the lungs, and to the diaphragm. Notice your chest and belly expand. On the exhale, follow the breath's journey back up through the body and out the nose. As you repeat this practice two more times, tune in to the experience of your body settling and feeling more grounded. Acknowledge any thoughts, emotions, or sensations you may feel during these three mindful breaths.

If possible, aim to practice three mindful breaths once each hour. This can be done by setting a timer or using reminders on your phone or computer. If you're lucky enough to live near a church, you might hear its bells at the beginning of each hour. Practicing this habit will help you feel centered in your body and bring you peace when you're feeling unsettled.

Breaking Bad Habits

The bad habits ahead—sitting too much and ignoring the body—are deeply embedded behaviors in most people's lives, mine included.

The process of breaking a bad habit begins when we sincerely assess the negative impact the bad habit is having and what benefits would result from breaking it. Often the impact will be measured in years, not in moments. Sitting for several hours at a time for one day is inconsequential. But sitting constantly all day, every day for years, maybe decades, will have a huge impact. When you take a broader view of your bad habits, you'll notice their significance not only on today but on your entire life.

Remember, it's much easier to replace a habit than to break it. Breaking habits takes willpower, which can run short when you're tired or unmotivated. But when you can find ways to swap out bad habits with healthier ones, you no longer need to depend so much on your resolve and grit.

Sitting Too Much

In his book *Get Up!: Why Your Chair Is Killing You and What You Can Do About It*, James Levine describes a nationwide epidemic of chair addiction, a constant need that's grown over the past century to incessantly sit. Our sedentary lifestyle is contributing to skyrocketing increases in diabetes, heart disease, and more. Some even say that sitting is the new smoking.

Addiction, whether to chocolate or a chair, is often a habit with a really satisfying reward. We get addicted to the way an action makes us feel in the moment, and this short-term payoff, left unchecked, guides us to repeat unhealthy behaviors over and over.

According to Levine, the average American sits for 13 hours each day. Let's replace some of those hours with movement. For starters, learn to use the pedometer on your smartphone or get an inexpensive pedometer ($10). Knowing how many steps you're already taking each day and then setting your sights on gradually reaching a 10,000-step goal will give you something tangible to shoot for.

After a few days of tracking your steps, you'll likely begin to notice that 10,000 steps–or maybe even 5,000 steps or 2,000 steps–simply aren't possible without some new habits. Try adding a morning or evening walk to your day. Create the practice of walking or pacing each time you're on a phone call. Park farther from a store's entrance when you're running errands. As you replace sitting with walking or even standing, you'll weaken the habit of constantly veering toward a chair.

Ignoring the Body

The body speaks to you in innumerable—and not always pleasant—ways. Through big and small signals, it grabs your attention so you can tend to its needs. And yet it's incredibly easy to create a habit of ignoring the body. Whether it's putting off a meal or a bathroom break, disregarding an urge to stretch or walk, or ignoring thirst, fatigue, or discomfort, almost everyone has been guilty of being a poor caretaker of their body.

When you frequently ignore your body's requests, you become disconnected. This fractured relationship can cause you to unconsciously mistreat yourself. Neglect and carelessness repeated daily over a lifetime have countless consequences for your health. The body is essential to your survival, and the extent to which you care for or disregard it will directly determine your well-being.

The good habits presented in this chapter all aim to help you become more connected to your body. When you are present in your body, you begin to cultivate a sense of companionship and kindness toward yourself. Breaking the habit of ignoring the body is achieved partly by building the good habits in this chapter, but it's also achieved through daily acknowledgment of vitality that comes with a healthy, well-cared-for body.

Tracking Your Progress

Use this tracker as a tool to help you monitor your progress and gain insight into why a habit perhaps isn't quite sticking. The purpose of tracking your habits is to help yourself learn, modify, and improve.

HABIT	M	T	W	TH	F	SAT	S

KEY TAKEAWAYS

- When you are present in the body, you are able to attune to your physical needs and emotions.
- Healthy habits that focus on your inner world provide the gateway to better self-care and a sense of solidarity with yourself.
- A 30-second stop and drop or a three-minute body scan can give you the opportunity to quickly check in with your inner state and triage your physical and emotional needs.
- Simple activities, such as walking, washing your hands, and breathing, can become moving meditations when you bring your intention and attention to them.
- Bad habits, such as sitting too much or ignoring the body, can be mindfully replaced with healthy habits. Replacing habits is easier than breaking them.

CHAPTER 4

Being Present While Eating

When was the last time you truly paid attention to the food on your plate? Eating is such a sensory experience, and yet we often barely notice flavors, aromas, and textures of the food we eat. Much of the time, eating is a mindless, automatic, unconscious activity.

The five habits in this chapter are designed to bring more presence to the act of nourishing yourself. Food is something to be relished, and mindful eating can lead to choosing food that is healthier. The adoption of mindful eating habits, and the elimination of a few mindless ones, have the potential to transform mealtimes and your relationship with food.

Mindful Eating

While many unhealthy eating habits are often attributed to *what* people eat, *how* people eat should also be examined. Hunger is a powerful cue, and cravings are compelling motivators. Furthermore, eating is a highly automated activity. Just as Pavlov's dogs showed us, the sight of food or the feeling of hunger triggers an unconscious response, which in the human realm can lead to mindless eating. Since we are pulled to food over and over, all day every day, it's easy to see why the brain habituates eating patterns and why we so rarely notice them.

Eating habits certainly have strings attached. Whether it's wasting food, overeating, making unhealthy choices, skipping meals, mistaking thirst for hunger, or simply eating out of boredom, most of us have a few food habits we'd be better served without.

But good habits, ones that flood the act of eating with presence and gratitude, are accessible antidotes. As you learn to bring consciousness to your behaviors with food, you begin to tune in to this delicious, nourishing, and often delightful facet of living. Mindful eating to nourish, satiate, and satisfy yourself is an act of self-love and a necessary component of your well-being and happiness.

Building Healthier Habits

Eating habits, like eating around the same time each day, in the same place, and with the same people, make mindful eating an ideal activity for habit stacking. When you pair a new habit you want to establish with an existing habit, you are habit stacking. This is a particularly effective way to build habits because you group positive activities together, so each action cues the next. This is how effective routines are built.

For example, if you wanted to establish the habit of sharing three things you're grateful for each day, stacking this activity on top of your nightly family mealtime allows dinner to prompt the gratitude discussion. You are reminded to do the new habit before, after, or alongside a pre-existing habit.

Using the ingrained habit of mealtime to anchor new mindfulness habits, you can begin to learn to pay attention to the moment and to the act of meeting your own needs through food. This attention gives you the space to notice things like your hunger, satiation, preferences, and aversions as well as the sensory nuances of eating. Flavors come alive. You tune in to how your food makes you feel. Eating becomes a celebration rather than a chore or struggle.

Pause Before Eating

Saying grace is a beautiful way to create a moment of pause and presence before eating. But for those who don't subscribe to a particular religion, this prayer practice can feel out of alignment. About 12 years ago, my friend Patrick lived in our home for a short time, and we soon witnessed his mealtime pause every time we ate together. Patrick simply closed his eyes, hovered his open hands a few inches above his food, and silently thanked those who had a part in bringing it to his plate. The spirit

of gratitude he evoked with his mindful pause was conta-
gious and set the tone for the entire meal.

As you sit down to eat, before you pick up your
fork, gently close your eyes or soften your gaze. Relax.
If it aligns for you, place your hands over your heart,
raise them a few inches above your food, or bring your
palms together in prayer. For a breath or two, turn your
awareness to your appetite, noticing what it feels like to
experience hunger. Then take a few grateful breaths, perhaps reciting the phrase "thank you" in your mind. Smile,
open your eyes, and begin to eat.

As you begin to establish this practice, it might help
to place a written "pause" reminder at your place at the
table. You might also set the table with everything upside
down as a cue to pause before you begin. As you develop
this habit, you will feel an increasing awareness, enjoy-
ment, and appreciation of your food.

Take Three Mindful Bites

My family and I eat most dinners together at our house.
Depending on the day, sometimes we all arrive at the
table absolutely ravenous. Our pattern is to start shoveling food into our mouths the moment we grab our forks.
In our rush to feed ourselves, we miss out on the utter
delight of the first few bites of our meal.

The first few bites are special. The brain loves novelty,
and your first few forkfuls, especially of a new food, light up
the mind and engage the taste buds. The trouble is, as you
adapt to the pleasure, the novelty wears off, and the food
becomes less and less enjoyable. Bringing awareness to
your first three bites is like winning the food lottery.

As you prepare to eat, take a grounding inhale; then exhale and drop into the moment. Place a small amount of food in your mouth, close your eyes, and slowly begin to chew. What do you notice about the flavor, aroma, and texture of what you are eating? How do the taste buds, body, and mind respond to your food? Notice every aspect of this experience as you repeat these mindful bites two more times.

As you begin to solidify this habit, consider swapping out your fork for a spoon. This will this serve as a visual reminder, and you'll have to be more mindful as you eat. Your reward is the pleasure that savoring the first three bites brings you.

Practice Gratitude

Your food may travel hundreds of miles and pass through many hands before it arrives on your plate. The labor that's required before your meal reaches the table is astonishing. *Thanks A Thousand* by A. J. Jacobs chronicles the author's mission to personally thank every person who had a hand in his morning coffee. The book put into perspective how much effort and how many people are behind what we eat. While mealtime can be something we take for granted, it can also become a catalyst for moments of deep gratitude and reverence.

As you enjoy your food, take a few moments to think of where it came from and who played a part in the process of getting it to you. If you are eating with others, take turns acknowledging two or three people who have contributed to the meal. Pay your compliments to the cook in detail rather than simply saying, "This is good." Let the feeling of gratitude settle and permeate.

I've learned that writing down the things we're thankful for is the best way to support a gratitude practice. Place a pen and small notebook at your table so you can document at least one person along the food chain you're thankful for at each meal. Your reward for this practice is a broadening of your perspective about how your food arrives at your table and an increased appreciation for the people—close by or far away—whose labor puts food on your table.

Do a Hunger Scan

I had the pleasure of interviewing Michelle Babb, author of *Mastering Mindful Eating*, on my *60 Mindful Minutes* podcast, and I'll never forget this advice from her: "Eat your food, feel your feelings." As Michelle explained, people have physiological hunger (the body's need for fuel) and emotional hunger, which is our psychological need to feel calm, safe, and cared for. If you're not mindful, eating can be an attempt to satisfy your emotional needs by comforting yourself with food.

This is why tuning in to your hunger's true nature is pivotal. When you can recognize that some of the body's cravings are actually emotional cravings born from anxiety or sadness, you can tend to those emotional needs without food.

Before you reach for a snack or begin to prepare a meal, sit for a moment and close your eyes. Bring your attention to your hunger. Where are you feeling it? How would you describe it? What else are you feeling? Take a minute to investigate the source of your hunger to be sure you're eating for the right reasons. If you discover that emotions are at the heart of your hunger, inquire within yourself how you could tend to those emotions. Some ideas include deep breathing, stretching, movement, journaling, or reaching out to a friend.

The cue for this habit is feeling hungry when it is not your regular meal or snack time—for example, in the late afternoon or after you've already eaten dinner. The reward is increased awareness of what your body needs.

Chew 10 Times

America is a country of quick eaters. In fact, according to data published by the Organisation for Economic Co-operation and Development, Americans are some of the fastest eaters on the planet, clocking only about 60 minutes of daily dining time, while people in France, Italy, Greece, and Spain spend twice that amount.

When you rush to get through meals instead of relishing them, you skip over a crucial aspect of digestion: chewing. Chewing not only helps you break down food and absorb nutrients but also helps you slow down the eating process so your body has time to register fullness. Even more important, slowing down to truly savor your meal allows you to appreciate its flavors and to connect more deeply with the people you're eating with.

Opinions vary somewhat, but on the whole, it's recommended that you chew each bite 20 to 40 times. That's much easier said than done. Start with just 10 chews per bite or you may get frustrated and stop bothering. Take a bite, put down your fork, and count your chews. As you repeat this practice, you can drop the counting and simply tune in to the joy of eating and tasting.

This habit is a challenge to return your attention to each and every bite. Putting down your fork will make the formation of the habit easier. The stacked habit sequence looks like this: *After you put down your fork, you will chew your food 10 times.* When you take the time to slow down and thoroughly chew your food, you savor your food more and may even notice that your overall digestion process improves.

Breaking Bad Habits

Eating mindlessly is a bad habit worth breaking for so many reasons. Health books will tell you that when you thoughtlessly and carelessly eat, you tend not to be very discerning about your food choices. Perhaps you eat too much in one sitting, eat too often, or eat for the wrong reasons. Those are helpful insights, but for the purposes of this book, let's focus on why mindless eating impacts the joy of eating.

When my family first moved to our new home in Florida, we discovered that someone had planted the crown of a pineapple in the dirt near our shed. Being from Canada, I had never seen a pineapple grow before, and I was enamored with the process. Here's what's incredible about pineapples: they take over a year to grow, and each plant produces only one single fruit. By the time our little pineapple was ready to pick, it was like harvesting a rare diamond. My husband and I sliced it open and savored it like it was the most precious thing we'd ever eaten.

Food is amazing when you really think about it. But it's easy to miss out on awe and wonder when you engage in mindless eating habits.

Preloading Your Fork

When I asked my friend Sarah Geha, a certified nutrition specialist with a master of science degree in nutrition and integrative health, her best advice on mindful eating was this: stop preloading your fork. Many people have the habit of immediately refilling their fork after they've placed food in their mouth. This hurried and mindless shoveling of food into the mouth precludes the sensory experience of eating.

Sarah suggests that after you take a bite, you place the fork back down on the table until you have completely finished chewing what's in your mouth. When you treat each bite like its own event, you create enough space between your bites to be able to maintain awareness of the process of eating. This allows you to be present to the body's signals and to the food itself. With the fork placed on the table between bites, you can ask yourself: What am I enjoying about this bite? What am I noticing about my body's response to this food? What about this process of eating can I find delightful, even miraculous?

Putting the fork down between bites can be a challenging habit to start if your automated way of preloading the fork is deeply wired. Practice using your nondominant hand to lift and guide your fork. See if this helps remind you to replace your fork after each bite and stay focused on the act of eating and the sensations that accompany it.

Distracted Eating

In a world full of gadgets that both facilitate work and provide entertainment, it's no wonder that being fully present during meals is difficult. In our mindlessness, we are prone to multitask while eating, and smartphones are making this bad habit even more prevalent. Look around at a restaurant and you'll notice many diners are on their phones.

When you think about the mindful eating habits outlined in this chapter and how they can turn every meal into a moment of joy, it's easy to see how distracted eating is kryptonite to delighted eating.

Mealtime ought to be sacred space. An undistracted 30 minutes to eat gives you the chance to deliberately connect to your food, your body, and your dining companions. As your awareness is sharpened, you will learn to listen, trust, and respect yourself more fully.

Start by making the commitment to eat your meals at a table versus on the couch in front of the television or at your desk in front of the computer. Create a dining space that's inviting by making sure the table is clear of clutter. Add attractive place mats and cloth napkins, and consider placing a vase filled with fresh flowers on the table.

Then institute a no-technology rule for mealtimes and strictly enforce it. Move devices to another room. Whether you're eating alone or with others, be present and engaged. Contemplate thought-provoking questions or engage others in conversation. Use mealtime as a way to reinhabit yourself and your life.

Tracking Your Progress

Use this tracker as a tool to improve your eating habits and bring joy to your meals. Look to increase positive habits and decrease negative ones. Celebrate your progress!

HABIT	M	T	W	TH	F	SAT	S

KEY TAKEAWAYS

- Mindful eating helps you make healthier, more discerning food choices, but it also allows you to savor the sacred act of eating.
- Well-being is impacted by not only what you eat but *how* you eat.
- Habits that prompt you to pause, slow down, chew more, and eat with gratitude allow you to create a better relationship with food and eating.
- Eliminating bad habits, such as preloading your fork and being distracted while eating, can help you eat more mindfully.
- Nourishing yourself mindfully is an act of self-love.

CHAPTER 5

Being Present in Relationships

Unless you move to a cave or a remote island, chances are you'll spend much of your life in relationships with other human beings. Navigating each other's personalities, beliefs, and preferences isn't easy. Without a doubt, relationships are the most challenging aspect of life, but they're also the most meaningful. In this chapter, you'll learn habits that will help you more mindfully connect with the people you care about. When you interact with friends, family, and colleagues with awareness, you'll see your capacity for love, kindness, and connection grow.

Mindful Connection

A key health and longevity indicator is the presence of strong, loving relationships. In 2005, *National Geographic* published an article titled "The Secrets of Long Life" that discussed Blue Zones and the possible reasons why clusters of people in certain places live longer-than-average lives. One explanation for these people's longevity was that they ate well, but they also loved well. Study after study has shown that healthy social networks are critical to well-being. Conversely, disharmony and loneliness lead to chronic illness and depression.

Humans are wired for connection with others. The powerful urge to belong—to be accepted and loved—is in our biology. Regardless of how confident or self-conscious you are, how introverted or extroverted, you need some degree of healthy connection in your life. Without this innate drive to connect, support each other, and procreate, humans would be extinct by now. Relationships are a central facet of our lives because we simply cannot exist without them.

When you start to relate to people in your life with more awareness, you increase your capacity for kindness, patience, and compassion, which are the cornerstones of harmonious connections. When you begin to relate more harmoniously, your social bonds strengthen. No doubt your life is a tapestry of relationships. When you strengthen them through mindful connection, life becomes more meaningful, fulfilling, and vibrant.

Building Healthier Habits

Our lives are the sum of our habits. Relationships involve habits, too, and these habits directly affect how connected and congruent you feel. Want better relationships? Build better relationship habits.

Being more mindful in your relationships is achieved by developing practices that help you become more aware in your day-to-day interactions with the people in your life. Habits that snap you out of your mindless automation allow you to be more present and see more clearly. When I am present with my husband Marc, our kids, my friends, and even the cashier at the grocery store, I become aware of my own way of being, how I'm showing up in the interaction, and how that impacts the other person. Mindful habits help me be more responsible and less reactive with those around me.

Life feels good when your relationships are in good working order. When you are feeling warmly connected to those around you and you're able to create less conflict, life feels better. As you use your awareness to invest in your relationships and to navigate them more consciously, your relationships simply work better. The following habits are designed to support your efforts.

Listen to Appreciate

When someone is speaking, it's not uncommon to be calculating your response and waiting for your opening to reply. But that's hearing, not listening. To listen means to absorb what someone says, to contemplate it, and to reflect it back to the speaker. It's motivated by a desire to know and understand the person who's speaking rather than to be known and understood yourself. Listening to appreciate means that you're not only attempting to comprehend the speaker but you're engaged in and value what they are saying.

Listening to appreciate takes *lots* of practice. When someone initiates a conversation with you, note the opportunity to exercise this new skill. You may even tell the person that you intend to listen from a place of appreciation. When the person is done expressing their thought, take a breath before speaking and then begin with a phrase like "What I appreciate about what you said is . . ." Once you feel you have adequately captured and valued what was said, make your contribution to the conversation by saying, "What I'd add is . . ." Of course, this will initially feel clunky and awkward, but by using your own words and practicing frequently, it will begin to feel more natural.

Share your commitment to creating better listening habits with a few people in your life. Each time you interact with these people, the accountability you've created will serve as a reminder to practice this habit. Don't be afraid to ask them for feedback on how you are doing. Any conversation can serve as an effective cue for this behavior, and the feedback, even if constructive, is a positive reward.

Ask Two Questions

People feel most connected to others when they feel seen, heard, and understood. The feeling of being understood and appreciated, in joy and in struggle, helps create a deep sense of belonging and security.

Ironically, the people we are closest to are usually the ones we are least curious about. We already "know" our loved ones and closest friends, so it's easy to overlook opportunities to go deeper. We tend to go through the motions with people we spend our lives with rather than seek out opportunities to see each other with fresh eyes and an inquisitive heart.

Several years ago, one of Marc's clients shared with him a daily practice that she and her husband had started, which resulted in them feeling profoundly connected to each other. They each asked and answered two specific questions, which created an opportunity to share with the other meaningful and noteworthy aspects of their day.

The simple practice goes like this. Take turns asking and answering these two questions: What would you have me know about your life? What would you like to be acknowledged for? Notice how these questions prompt responses that will provide the opportunity to go into more depth than if you had simply asked, "How was your day?" Practice this habit with anyone in your life, including family, friends, and colleagues, to create openings to know others more deeply.

Pick one person in your life to solidify this habit with. Use routine moments in your day, such as mealtimes or right before bed, to anchor this ritual into your life. The reward for this habit is deepening your connection with another person and feeling contentment about that relationship.

Consider the 10,000 Reasons

Other humans, even if you love them, can sometimes be irritating. It's easy to be frustrated when someone is late, takes up an extra parking spot, responds to you curtly, or doesn't respond all. These types of behaviors may leave you feeling simultaneously perplexed and infuriated. You may ask: Why the heck did they do that? What's wrong with them?

When you're filled with judgment and anger, you're unlikely to seek to understand others' behavior, and as a result, disconnection flourishes. The truth is, you often don't *really* know what motivates people to behave in certain ways. There could be 10,000 reasons. An individual's collection of past experiences, beliefs, worldviews, and desires creates countless motives for their actions.

The practice of 10,000 reasons goes like this: When someone does something you dislike or can't understand, greet their behavior with a sense of curiosity. Begin by mentally composing a list of reasons why they did what they did. Maybe it has something to do with how they were raised or a negative experience they had years ago. Maybe they're going through something really stressful or haven't had enough to eat today. You'll find that by the time you explore three or four possible reasons, you've already started to shift from judgment to compassion.

Use the time when you're winding down before bed to reflect on the day's interactions, noting any moments when someone's behavior was perplexing or frustrating, and write down how you could see it differently. This habit will offer you a new sense of interconnectedness and ease with other people.

Give a Long Hug

Hugs are healthy. Even a quick squeeze unleashes a cocktail of good-feeling chemicals, like serotonin, oxytocin, and dopamine. If you can hold on for 20 seconds or more, you'll also decrease the flow of the stress hormone cortisol, thereby helping the body return to a sense of safety and calm.

It's easy to take a hug for granted and forget to be present for it. When I meet up with a friend or give a quick goodbye to Marc, I can automate the embrace. But when I create a commitment to truly tune in to a hug and drop into the experience with awareness and intention, something shifts. The longer the embrace, the calmer and more connected I feel.

Hugs typically last just a few seconds. The next time you find yourself in a position to hug someone you know well, ask them (before the hug) if they'd mind if you held it for 20 to 30 seconds instead. Perhaps explain how a big, long hug releases feel-good chemicals and helps you feel connected. Of course, this will likely feel awkward, even silly, at first. But as you hug, and the more often you practice, the better it will feel.

Stack this habit with the liftoffs and landings habit that follows. Start to see yourself as a world-class hugger. Your renewed sense of calm and connection will help make this behavior a habit.

Practice Liftoffs and Landings

When our daughters were still in diapers, Marc and I met Carrie Contey, an extraordinary parenting coach. One practice she taught that has always stuck with me is the habit of mindful liftoffs and landings.

When you leave home, even for just a quick errand, do you holler across the house, or do you take a moment to make eye contact with other people in your household and tell them you're leaving and when you'll be back? When you arrive back home, do you take a moment to reconnect, or do you just go about your business? Taking a minute to connect with the people you live with gives them the sense that they matter to you. It's a small gesture that helps the people you share your life with feel valued.

Before you depart the house, find the others in your household and let them know, face-to-face, that you're leaving. If it's appropriate, put a hand on their shoulder or give them a quick hug. You might say, "I'm headed out for a bit. I wanted to check in with you before I left." When you return, seek them out again and tell them you're home.

For the next few weeks, practice mindful departures and arrivals each time you come and go from home. Let the people you share your life with know that you're trying to make this change and that you're working on this new habit. You will be rewarded by feeling a greater sense of belonging.

Breaking Bad Habits

When it comes to improving relationships, people tend toward a 50/50 approach: in other words, "I'll try if you try" or "Let's meet halfway." The trouble with this approach is that you spend a lot of energy eyeing the other person's effort instead of focusing on your own. As a recovered score keeper (well, almost recovered), I can attest to how connection eludes me when I am waiting for someone else to do better rather than focusing solely on the one thing I can change: my own behavior.

Not all relationships are healthy, and some should definitely have you walking in the other direction. But much of the time, a "good enough" relationship just needs one person's heartfelt intention for it to tip in a positive direction.

I bring this up because as you seek to eliminate your bad relationship habits, it's easy to start pointing out how others can improve, too. If there is one thing I have learned in life, it's that the best way to effect change is to model new behavior.

It takes an incredible amount of humility to look honestly at your bad relationship habits and seek to alter or eliminate them. But when you take responsibility for your own actions and patterns, your efforts not only result in your own growth but also inspire others.

Distracted Listening

Worse than listening to respond is not listening at all. I see this most often in myself when it comes to my kids. When they begin chattering away, especially if it's about a video game or something they saw on YouTube, I can be unquestionably guilty of inadvertently tuning them out. On my computer, reading a book, prepping dinner, or just lost in my own thoughts, I'm there in body, but my mind is elsewhere.

While they may not say anything, people absolutely know it when you're only half listening to them. And even though such an infraction seems inconsequential in the moment, constantly leaving someone to feel unheard or unseen can be toxic to a relationship. When you show others the respect and consideration of your full attention, however, you convey through your behavior that you value and appreciate what they have to say.

When someone begins speaking to you, pause for a moment to either stop what you're doing or ask them to wait until you're done. People would much rather you say, "Hang on, let me just finish typing this email so I can be done and really listen to what you're saying," than to stand there talking away when you're not even looking at them. Commit to making full eye contact when you're engaged in listening. Move your body to face the person who is speaking, put down what's in your hands, and give them your full attention. If you find your mind wandering, pull your attention back to the present moment.

Displaying Contempt

Few behaviors are more toxic to a relationship than displays of contempt, such as eye-rolling, sneering, and sarcasm. According to renowned researcher John Gottman, displays of contempt are the number one predictor of divorce. Seemingly innocent enough, these constant little digs drive a serious wedge between people.

I'd imagine that most people in a loving relationship would not want to have a habit that constantly left their partner, friend, or relative feeling devalued. But this is the tricky thing about an eye-rolling habit or the tendency to undercut someone. As habits, these behaviors live outside our awareness. The best way to combat them is to bring them into full view.

One of the most difficult questions you could ever ask someone is "What is it like to be in a relationship with me?" When you give someone the permission and space to honestly share their experience and speak without you being defensive, you can learn so much about yourself and how others perceive you. It might not be easy to hear what a friend, child, or spouse has to say, but on the other side of their disclosure is an opportunity to change how you show up in the relationship.

Tracking Your Progress

If a habit doesn't stick right away, it usually only needs some modifications or tweaks to get it just right.

HABIT	M	T	W	TH	F	SAT	S

KEY TAKEAWAYS

- Relationships contribute to your well-being when they are harmonious and fulfilling. Mindfulness helps you be more compassionate, patient, and kind.
- Relationship habits, such as improving how you listen and being more intentional in how you connect, make relationships stronger.
- While breaking bad relationship habits takes humility and practice, it's worth the effort to have better relationships.

CHAPTER 6

Mindfulness at Work

While the stakes might feel higher at work—especially when pressure, deadlines, and dollars are in play—the truth is that no matter what your role, everyone has a need to be valued and feel accomplished. Mindfulness at work isn't some woo-woo ambition for hippies; it's a tool you can deliberately employ to create collaborative connections, reduce stress, and feel good about what you do. If you're like most people, you will spend up to a third of your life working, and that time has an undeniable impact on your quality of life. The habits ahead aim to make those hours more peaceful and productive.

Mindful Work

Work is fertile ground for discontent. If you meet Monday morning with a sense of gloom, even dread, work life can be a source of angst, disappointment, stress, and dissatisfaction. But you owe it to yourself to not simply endure decades of work in order to get to retirement when you can "really start living." There's no such thing as a happiness layaway plan; you are meant to feel happy and fulfilled today.

In the pursuit of a more mindful life, it's important to place as much emphasis, maybe even more emphasis, on *how* you do what you do versus *what* you do, or the results you produce. Your disposition and approach to work impacts not only how you feel but how you make others feel.

How you work also, inevitably, impacts your results. Research published in *JAMA: The Journal of the American Medical Association* found that mindfulness programs can help reduce stress. Mindfulness can also improve focus and concentration. When you're less stressed and more focused, you make better decisions, are better able to access your creativity, and generally get along better with others. For the sake of your work quality and the quality of your work relationships, it truly makes a difference to bring mindfulness habits to the office.

Building Healthier Habits

Through healthy work habits like those in this chapter, you can build a work life strategically designed to decrease stress, overload, and disharmony. Healthy work habits help you do what you need to do at work and ensure that you show up as your best self in the process. When your habits cultivate presence and awareness and reduce the time you spend working and interacting mindlessly, what you do and how you do it improve. You also get better at recognizing and enforcing your work-life boundaries.

When you begin to look at work not simply as a place to get things done and earn money but as a place to grow and evolve, your intentions related to your tasks and your team change. For example, perhaps you have intentions to treat others kindly and to grant space for differing opinions. Knowing that confrontation, pressure, and overcommitment make it easy for you to slip into a self-focused, achievement-oriented state can also help you recognize that your good intentions may get overshadowed if you haven't cultivated a system for keeping them present. This is why it's important both to create intentions for how you want to work as well as to put your efforts into creating healthier work habits.

Establish Mindful Work Pauses

People who get a lot done are celebrated in the Western work world; our culture prizes "doing" far more than it values "being." The power to overcome this strong cultural pull comes when you habituate activities that help you be more present and when you see that creativity, collaboration, and states of flow are not only far easier to access but also more beneficial to your overall well-being.

When you are in a relaxed, open, and mindful state, you can better regulate yourself; you can see more clearly; you can prioritize more effectively; and you can relate to others with more patience, humility, and kindness. Conversely, in a mindless state, you weaken your ability to manage yourself and are consumed with managing tasks, deadlines, outcomes, and other people. Deliberately planning mindful work pauses between tasks is critical for cultivating greater awareness, relaxation, and openness.

Using a tool such as a timer, smartphone reminder, calendar alert, or hourly chime establishes a cue that will serve as a prompt to pause periodically throughout your day. Upon hearing the cue, stop what you're doing, take a few mindful breaths, and ask yourself these questions: How do I feel? What could I shift? What is my state? Who am I being in this moment?

It's easy to grow immune to reminder prompts, such as those outlined earlier. As you build your anchor for this pausing habit, aim to switch it up from week to week. Otherwise, you may find yourself ignoring your cue. Set an intention to be fully aware during this practice. Your reward is a meaningful reconnection with yourself as well as the self-confidence that comes with the ability to redirect and regulate your behavior.

Take Lunch Breaks

Lunch breaks are becoming a rarity. A study conducted by OnePoll found that 51 percent of Americans feel that a lunch break is rare and unrealistic, with 30 percent of study respondents reporting that they regularly opt to eat lunch at their desk instead. For those who do take a break, the lunch "hour" is basically a dinosaur at this point.

Breaking for lunch can feel like an unproductive indulgence when you don't see or understand the benefit it provides. Besides offering an opportunity to refuel your body, the mental rest you give yourself during a lunch break can improve performance capacity, boost your mood, and increase your energy, according to the American Psychological Association.

A healthy life is less like a marathon and more like a series of sprints. You're not designed to continuously, day after day, slog on and on until you drop. You're meant to distribute your energy reserves with alternating sprints and rests throughout the day. Pauses to rest and refuel are what give you the power and stamina to do your best work.

Take a lunch break. Leave your workspace and eat with colleagues. Practice some of the mindful eating habits from chapter 4. Go for a walk outside. Read a book. Close your eyes and feel your body wind down. Aim for at least a 30-minute break.

Find a colleague who can serve as both your lunch date and accountability partner. If this is a new or challenging habit, start by committing to just one day a week and grow from there. Your reward is giving your mind a rest and finding a sense of calm and ease.

Be Mindful about Meetings

Oh, meetings. Aimless, unproductive, too numerous, and frequently contentious, meetings have become an all-too-common problem that can make anyone feel frustrated, stressed, and dispirited in the workplace. Furthermore, the encroachment of meetings leads to a stressful scramble to protect yourself as well as your time, position, and ideas while you try to find the space to simply do the work you were hired to do.

It's easy to forget that work life is not so different from family life. In both settings, there is an interconnected group of people who want to feel valued and purposeful. When you meet with others and have a clear focus for your time together *and* a clear intention for your way of being (open, curious, and nonjudgmental, for example), you are more capable of charting a productive and peaceful course for the meeting.

Create a template for your meetings that answers these three questions: What is the focus of this meeting? What will this meeting accomplish? What is my intended way of being? Print it out and spend five minutes before each meeting answering these questions. While this process may not change the dynamics of the meeting, especially if you're not the meeting organizer, you have an opportunity to change the way *you* navigate meetings by bringing yourself more mindfully to the process. Your reward is being more centered and grounded while you're in meetings and perhaps even helping yourself or your team avoid unnecessary meetings.

Create a five-minute appointment with yourself before each meeting in your calendar so that you can do this prework before the meeting begins. Use a meeting alert to jog your memory. Print out the templates so they're handy.

Reduce Distractions

If given unlimited access to your attention, phones, email inboxes, and colleagues can be an endless source of interruption, making it seemingly impossible to get anything done. According to research into digital distraction by the University of California, Irvine, it takes us about 25 minutes to refocus on a task after an interruption. Repeated dozens, maybe hundreds of times each day, it's no wonder so many people feel unproductive and stressed.

The antidote I've used for two decades is distraction-free time blocking. When I protect blocks of time from interruption, my productivity and focus soar. With my office door closed, my phone in do-not-disturb mode, and my email turned off, I am able to give the task at hand—like writing this book—my single-minded attention.

Work is one place where you share your gifts with the world. It's critical to tackle the distractions that stand in the way of your ability to share those gifts. Go through your calendar and schedule time for specific tasks, such as projects you're working on or administrative tasks you need to plow through. Treat this block like an appointment with yourself and make yourself inaccessible to others. Turn off all distractions and close your office door. This behavior will be reinforced and rewarded with the ability to easily reach a state of flow, with fewer of the costly restarts that occur after a distraction and an increased ability to get things done.

Stack this habit with the following habit of creating the closing-time ritual. Time block your day (or week) as part of your planning process.

Create a Closing-Time Ritual

It's easy to fall prey to the illusion of completion, or the idea that if you just keep working, you will finally be done. Let's be honest—most work is never done. And just as you think it is, it starts all over again. *You* decide when work is done, not the work itself. Intentionally creating clear stopping points in your day is a practice that allows you to declare that you're done and it's time to turn off the engines and rest.

Mindfulness helps you put your work into perspective and see it as just one aspect of your life, not its solitary focus. Living to work is not living; it's a treadmill existence of mindlessly giving your days away instead of living them fully and intentionally. Mindfulness helps you maintain a healthy distance from your work so that your identity isn't wrapped up into what you do but is instead a reflection of who you are.

Create a closing-time ritual for the end of your workday. Make a plan for the next day and jot down any issues you'll tackle at that time. Power down your computer. Use your commute to transition from work mode. If you work from home, go for a "commute" walk around the block and change out of your day clothes. Put a "closed" sign on your office door. Turn off access to your email via your smartphone.

Set a time of day that is your firm stopping point. Create accountability by sharing this time with others. Your reward is a sense of completion at the end of each day and the strength that comes with the ability to create stronger boundaries between your work and home life.

Breaking Bad Habits

Mindless work habits can be hard to break for three reasons. First, they can be deeply rooted, especially for people who have been working for decades. Second, work–specifically repetitive work–produces a trance state, which is why it's so easy to lose yourself in your tasks and ambitions. In this automated zombie-like condition, the hours of your workday fly by. Finally, work isn't often seen as a place for practicing, or even discussing, things like mindfulness. Many people subscribe to the notion that personal growth is something to be done in the off-hours and neglect to see the opportunities to grow and evolve at work. While that's changing, mindfulness in the workplace is a reasonably new concept.

Two bad habits in particular–working at warp speed and multitasking–make it even harder to stay mindful. These two habits fan the flames of mindlessness because they challenge your ability to slow down and be fully present in what you're doing. Tackling these bad habits requires not only doing your work differently but also *thinking* differently about your work by acknowledging that your well-being is as important as your productivity.

Working at Warp Speed

For those of us in the habit of creating unrealistic to-do lists and taking on too many commitments at once, it seems that the only solution is to speed up. I am often guilty of this. In my frantic busyness, I am edgy and quick to be irritated by interruptions. I lose the parts of me that I value most: my centeredness, patience, self-compassion, and presence. This frenzied, frantic energy is a stark contrast to the energy of ease and calm that I prefer to bring to my work.

In my experience, I can work like either a bee or a butterfly. Have you ever noticed the difference? Bees work with a focused velocity of something that has a lot to do and not enough time to do it. Butterflies, on the other hand, float, flutter, and meander. And yet, in both cases, the job still gets done. Even at its peaceful pace, the butterfly does not starve.

The speed at which you approach your work directly impacts the level of mindfulness you can bring to it. When you're lost in crossing off one task after another, you can lose your connection to yourself and the intentions behind the work you're doing.

Integrate the breaking of this habit with the habit of mindfully pausing. Using timers and reminders to snap you out of your mindlessness, check in with your speed. Pause and slow down. Be a butterfly.

Multitasking

In a culture that celebrates productivity over presence, multitasking can make you feel efficient and effective. But something is lost when you're juggling more than one thing at a time: your full attention and awareness in the moment. When tasks are simple and don't require much discernment, self-regulation, or creativity, mindlessly multitasking can be fairly inconsequential. But when tasks are more complex—such as those in which you're interacting with others—the presence of too many tasks causes your thinking and attention to become divided and blunted.

You're your most productive when you focus on only one thing at a time. When we're multitasking, we're essentially just switching quickly between tasks. It's more accurate to call it task stacking, which actually makes you slower and less productive. In addition, it wires the brain to be less capable of single-minded focus and concentration.

I'm often reminded of the insights on washing dishes found in Thich Nhat Hanh's book *The Miracle of Mindfulness*. He recommends that whenever you are doing something—washing dishes, for example—only do that one task. Focus the mind and attention and bring the full breadth of awareness to each action and movement. The phrase "just wash the dishes" has become a helpful mantra for me to remember to do only one thing at a time.

Try it on. When you're doing something at work—typing an email, listening to a colleague, reviewing a report—mentally label the activity, bringing awareness to this singular action done with your full attention.

Tracking Your Progress

As you track your progress, note any adjustments you make, even if they are small changes. Also, note how new activities pair with other activities.

HABIT	M	T	W	TH	F	SAT	S

KEY TAKEAWAYS

- Mindfulness at work helps you create harmonious, collaborative connections; be less stressed; and feel more calm, focused, and productive.
- With healthy work habits you can reduce feelings work can sometimes cause, like being overwhelmed, discontent, and stressed.
- When your habits cultivate presence and awareness—and reduce the time you spend working and interacting mindlessly—what you do and how you do it improve.

CHAPTER 7

Mindful Stress Management

It's tough to be your best self when you have a lot of stress in your life. When you're steeped in fear and worry, the higher brain functions—discernment and amiability, for example—get less of the brain's resources, and the more primitive parts of the brain that focus on survival and protection take over.

The interesting thing about stress is that it's mainly caused by your reactions to what's happening rather than the event itself. And this is good news because it means that, although you can't always change what's happening externally, you can often change your response to it. In this chapter, you'll learn habits that increase your awareness of your stress responses and help you more gracefully navigate the hurdles stress can put in your path.

Mindful Stress Management

Stress is a normal part of living. The brain and the body are beautifully designed to handle life's ups and downs, respond quickly to crises, and rise to challenges with strength and tenacity. Stress can feel nerve-racking, like when you're late for a meeting, but it can also feel exhilarating and exciting, like being on a first date.

The trouble is stress has become a chronic, omnipresent force that can cause a constant state of disequilibrium. When you have too much coming at you and too few tools to minimize the impact, "stressed" becomes a default, or homeostatic, state. Remain this way for months, years, or even decades, and the body and mind will gradually erode, as evidenced by the massive increases in heart disease, sleep disorders, anxiety, depression, and weight gain over the past 50 years. Being chronically stressed is simply an unsustainable and unhappy way to live.

Balance is provided by the nervous system, which I like to think of as having two primary gears, depending on what your circumstances are asking of you. The sympathetic nervous system, or your "go mode," kicks in when you're faced with a challenge or a threat. Conversely, the parasympathetic system, or your "slow mode," kicks in when you're calm, resting, and digesting. The key to mindful stress management is to be aware when your sympathetic system is engaged and to actively and deliberately engage your parasympathetic system in order to restore equilibrium. In essence, you become the captain of the ship, mindfully steering your internal responses and navigating the choppy waters of life with awareness.

Building Healthier Habits

Habits that support stress management help you not only deal better with your circumstances in real time but also rewire the brain for more equanimity over the long term. Calm and grounded will steadily become your new default state, and you'll begin to develop a sensitivity to disequilibrium instead of it running unconsciously in the background of your life.

When you lack healthy stress-management strategies, you may find yourself leaning toward digital distraction to anesthetize yourself to the unpleasant effects of stress. But although it does numb the discomfort, it doesn't address the problem.

The true antidote to stress is to become aware of how you're feeling and appropriately redirect and reregulate yourself in healthier ways. When you establish and maintain healthy habits, such as those that follow, you become more resilient, and your ability to bounce back from challenges and adversity is bolstered.

Not all challenges are negative; often they facilitate growth and lead to important insights. As you employ this chapter's habits, you'll learn how to lessen the negative impact of stress and leverage its positive aspects. As the habits become routine, you'll begin to see that life is happening *for* you, not *to* you.

Put Hands on Heart

The first response to stress should be compassion. When a child falls and bumps her knee, we don't scold her or analyze the fall. We tend to her, take her in our arms, and soothe her. You deserve the same response when you are stressed. When you give yourself small moments of care and lovingly soothe and reinhabit yourself during the day, you increase your capacity for self-care and your tolerance for adversity. This experience of self-solidarity reduces your tendency to soldier on and increases your capacity to self-regulate.

I have author Courtney Carver to thank for the practice of hands on heart. Ever since I read about it in her book *Soulful Simplicity*, I've experienced countless moments of reconnection and realignment with myself. I think you will, too.

Take a seat and close your eyes or soften your gaze. Place your right hand over your heart or in the middle of your chest. You may also place the left hand on top of the right. Apply an appropriate amount of pressure so you can feel the weight of your hand. As the chest rises and falls with the breath, repeat a phrase, such as "it's okay" or "relax." Let a feeling of ease permeate before you go on with your day.

Connect this habit with something you do many times a day, such as going to the bathroom or refilling your water glass or coffee mug. Your reward is an enhanced sense of solidarity with yourself.

Trade Up

It's amazing what you hear when you slow down and listen to your thoughts. If you were to broadcast them when you're stressed, you might hear things like "I can't do this," "This is not going to work out," or "I should never have taken this on." Your thoughts affect how you feel, which impacts what you do and how you respond. But here's the good news: you are capable of listening to your inner dialogue *and* upgrading it.

I learned the concept of "trading up" from my friend Kim Ades, who founded Frame of Mind Coaching in Toronto, Canada. Essentially, you isolate a negative thought, such as "I am doomed to fail," and you trade it in for a *slightly* more positive one, such as "Even if I fail, I will survive." The idea isn't to be unrealistically positive but rather to choose a new thought that is both believable and elevating in an incremental climb.

Take out a piece of paper. Tuning in to your inner dialogue, write down your dominant thoughts and isolate one that's emitting stress. Notice how the body responds to it. Does your heart race? Do you feel sad or anxious? Now, write a few upgrades to the negative thought and feel which one lands as true for you. Create space for a different possibility. Continue climbing the ladder of better-feeling thoughts until you notice a shift in how you feel.

Practice this habit as part of a mindful pause or your lunch break, during your commute, or as part of your bedtime routine. You'll be rewarded by this practice by learning to guide and redirect your thinking.

Do Breath Work

The breath has an astonishing stabilizing power. By deliberately steadying and deepening your breathing, you can return a hijacked nervous system to equilibrium and begin to steer yourself back to calm. In a composed state, you have more access to higher brain functions and emotional regulation.

Box breathing is a great go-to practice for activating the parasympathetic nervous system and producing increased calm, concentration, and focus. When you're whipped up or triggered and you find yourself in need of a quick remedy, this practice can help shift your disposition in only a few minutes.

Sit comfortably and take a few grounding breaths to get focused. Close your eyes or soften your gaze. When you're ready, begin by inhaling to a count of four and then holding the breath for a count of four. Now, exhale for a count of four and hold again for four. Repeat for one to two minutes. Modify the count up or down to best serve your needs. For added relaxation, make the exhale count slightly longer than the inhale count. If holding the breath feels like too much, simply pause for a beat.

Schedule a breath break in your day and set an alert to remind you. Alternatively, you can add this practice to your morning or evening routine, perhaps making it the first thing you do when you wake up or the last thing you do before you fall asleep. You will be rewarded with a deep feeling of relaxation and steadiness.

Hold and Relax

Fear is a natural and necessary part of your emotional spectrum. In response to potential threats or hazards, it makes sense that you would feel trepidation or even alarm. But when fear is disproportionally present, it causes feelings of chronic anxiety and stress. This unease often manifests in the body as tension, or clenching and holding your muscles as if anticipating the need to suddenly run or fight.

In a mindless state, you might barely notice this clenching until it begins to produce pain, perhaps in your neck, shoulders, or upper back. But by mindfully attuning to the tension and working to release it, you can calm the body muscle by muscle.

Using a technique known as progressive muscle relaxation, choose an area of the body where you sense tension. As you slowly inhale, contract the muscles in that area like you would if you were very cold. Then, as you slowly exhale, release and relax the muscles. Move through each major muscle group of the body, including the upper and lower legs, buttocks, back, chest, and arms. You can even tense and relax your face. When you've traveled through the body, finish with a few mindful breaths and notice any shift you feel.

This is another practice best done once a day. Think about your day and start to see when you're in most need of a reset. Perhaps it's midday. If so, anchor this habit to your lunch break. Maybe it's as you transition from your work life to home life, in which case anchor this habit to your closing-time ritual from chapter 6 (page 76). This habit will make you feel relaxed, centered, and more connected to the self.

Practice RAIN

There are moments, days, or even months when life seems to hand you lemons. Suffering is an inevitable part of living, but rather than accept or turn toward life's woes and strife, it's common to choose distraction or self-soothing by using external influences. The truth is, you're better served using your own inner resources to right the ship.

Tapping into your inner resources when you're troubled might be new for you. And yet, when you learn to turn inward to find peace, you begin to experience your unlimited and always-accessible store of wisdom and strength. One way to access this inner resource is through the practice of RAIN. A cornerstone of Tara Brach's teachings, it's an acronym for:

RECOGNIZE

ALLOW

INVESTIGATE

NURTURE

The practice provides an opportunity to orient toward your inner world, bringing curiosity and acceptance as well as comfort and compassion to your distress in the moment.

Sit comfortably and take a few mindful breaths as you turn inward. What do you recognize, feel, and see in your experience in this moment? Make space for it and allow it to be present instead of pushing it away or resisting it. Investigate your experience with curious questioning. Where are the negative feelings located in your body? What has happened to produce these emotions or circumstances? Finally, bring some healing compassion to yourself. Evoke a spirit of kindness toward yourself before you continue on with your day.

When you find yourself waiting, on hold or in line somewhere, use this pause to practice RAIN, which will reward you with feelings of love and kindness.

Breaking Bad Habits

The habits in the previous section seek to help you be more aware of your innate stress-management abilities. In many cases, you have the power to deliberately change your relationship to what's happening around you in order to reduce the internal impact because you have control over your stress response.

You also have influence over how much stress you *allow* into your life in the first place. Sometimes you may create the conditions of your own mayhem. Stressful circumstances can be the by-product of decisions you've made or boundaries you've allowed to be crossed. If you are in a less stressed state, you have increased clarity and can modify your behavior accordingly.

Two bad habits I'd like to shine a spotlight on—having no white space and powering through—exacerbate stress. How much space you have and how hard you think you need to work are correlated with how overcommitted, overtasked, and overwhelmed you feel. For those in the habit of simply taking on more than they can reasonably handle, breaking these habits will lead toward a more manageable existence.

Having No White Space

White space is a term used in the design world to describe the unused or unmarked space left around illustrations and text. In everyday life, it's the gaps you deliberately create amid all of your "doing." Look at your calendar for today or think about the past few days, and take an inventory of how closely all of your to-dos and obligations butt up against each other. Do you see any white space?

In the race to get more done and to fit more in, you may have a tendency to plan things back-to-back, leaving no pause in between. Not only does this make for a frenzied way of life, but it leaves no room for mindful check-ins to pause and return to your awareness. When you're so fixated on the doing that you forget to consider your being, the key to reestablishing equilibrium is to intentionally design your days with scheduled bouts of space.

Begin by creating 5- to 10-minute buffers between your meetings and tasks. These can be scheduled into your calendar or written into your to-do list in between each task. While you're buffering, practice mindfulness habits from this book (such as a mindful pause), take a short stroll, or simply just sit for a few moments with your eyes closed. Notice how it feels to create more space in your day and not have every moment allocated for tasks, meetings, or obligations.

Powering Through

A common response to having too much to do or too many problems to solve is to knuckle down and power through. In mindlessness, it's easy to think that if you just keep your head down and keep going, you'll find the light at the end of the tunnel. But as I explained in chapter 6, there's always another tunnel.

It's misguided to think you can override or bypass your stress response long-term. It will ultimately lead to burnout. Your ongoing exposure to excessive stress, often at your own hands, eventually culminates in emotional, physical, and mental exhaustion. You may get sick, become totally disillusioned, or find yourself in mental or emotional crisis. This is avoidable when you break the habit of powering through your stress.

Start by assessing this tendency and the conditions under which it is likely to occur. Is it only sometimes, like when you're up against a deadline, or is this the way you work every day? If it's the latter, spend a few minutes in inquiry, perhaps writing in your journal. Why do you push yourself so hard? How is it that you end up with more to do than time to do it? What would it feel like to live with more ease and less intensity? The next time you fall into this pattern, step away from the task at hand and practice one of your mindfulness habits.

Tracking Your Progress

As your life changes—perhaps you move, get a new job, or move to a home office—you'll notice how these shifts impact your habits.

HABIT	M	T	W	TH	F	SAT	S

KEY TAKEAWAYS

- You can't always change what's happening in the world, but you can change your response to it.
- Stress is a normal part of living. The trouble is chronic stress can place you in a constant state of disequilibrium.
- Habits that improve your stress-management skills also increase your ability to bounce back from challenges and adversity.
- You can use habits, such as RAIN, breath work, and trading up, to reinhabit your inner world and restore your sense of calm throughout the day.
- When you break bad habits, you'll find that you become a friend to yourself rather than a heartless tyrant who disregards your own well-being.

CHAPTER 8

Digitally Mindful

Technology has become the bedrock of modern life, permeating nearly every aspect of our days and influencing how we work, connect, play, and even sleep. Our devices have filled our lives with convenience and delight—but also tremendous distraction. Our digital habits challenge our ability to focus and be present and are often at odds with our mindful intentions. But if the suggestion to throw away your devices causes a cold sweat, rest assured, you'll get no such advice in this chapter. To make changes, you simply need to modify your approach and cultivate habits for how to mindfully use technology and prevent it from using you.

Mindful Technology

Take a quick inventory of your world, and you're bound to see dozens of ways that technology has made life easier. The smartphone, in particular, is a device that has brought with it an enormous number of tools to facilitate efficiency, connection, and convenience. Helpful for doing everything, including ordering groceries, banking, mapping road trips, curating news, and chatting with friends and family, smartphones feel indispensable.

Unfortunately, within the smartphone's design and the apps it houses is sophisticated technology deeply informed by the science of creating habits. The technology that drives smartphones intentionally aims to produce unconscious, repetitive behavior. Consider how often you see, hear, or feel some kind of prompt—a notification lights up the screen, a pinging sound rings out, or the phone vibrates—and you automatically respond. The use of smartphones is, in large part, automatic, and most people have formed powerful habits related to their phones without even realizing it.

Part of the reason for this is that your attention is a profit center; social media companies, search engines, and app producers are deeply financially invested in pulling you back into a mindless habit loop of click, scroll, watch, or play. When you're in a mindless state, your devices will use you, triggering unconscious behaviors that may not be in your best interest. But when you interrupt this pull toward technology with awareness, intention, and deliberateness, you reassert control over the technology you use. When you are being mindful, you consciously use your device for a specific purpose and then have the wherewithal to put it away.

Building Healthier Habits

Bringing presence to your use of technology helps you use devices with more awareness. Let's take a look at your existing digital habits. Maybe you check your notifications at a stoplight while driving or sift through headlines on news websites between meetings. These digital pit stops may seem benign, but when you add them up over the day, the situation starts to feel grimmer.

In her book *How to Break Up with Your Phone: The 30-Day Plan to Take Back Your Life*, Catherine Price suggests dozens of ways to deliberately make your phone less central in your life—including deleting social media apps, turning off all notifications, and creating no-phone zones.

You can also take advantage of some of the recent smartphone functionality designed to support your efforts to digitally disconnect when you're driving or going to bed. For example, I have used my phone's Do Not Disturb function for years to eliminate all the beeps and buzzes that pull me away from the present moment.

Whatever strategies you employ, there's no question that, in order to combat your phone's very deliberate assault on your attention, you must battle it with intention and a clear strategy. The habits in this chapter will help you stage your own rebellion.

Create Tech-Free Time Blocks

Taking breaks from and limiting access to your devices are two ways you can begin to make them less present in your life. For example, you can commit to a time each day when you power down your phone and give yourself a rest from screens. One good time to do this is an hour before bedtime. You can leave your phone charging in another room so you can break the habit of turning to it as soon as you wake up, or use a regular old alarm clock to wake up and set your phone aside while you peacefully move through the first hour of your day. You can commit to blocks of connection time with the people you love, placing your phone in another room so you can give these moments your full attention. Creating boundaries like these will help you strengthen your independence from your devices and weaken their magnetic pull.

Create a few tech-free time blocks in your day. Begin by creating the habit of turning your phone off an hour before bed and keeping it off until an hour after you've awakened the next morning. See if you can set your device to automatically go into sleep mode at a certain time.

Set a timer to go off every evening about an hour before you go to bed to remind you to turn your device off. Place your device in another room or in a cupboard so it's out of sight. Once you've practiced this for a few days, you will begin to feel the reward: a sense of calm and an ability to see your reflexive tendencies more clearly.

Establish Device-Free Dinner

As you learned in chapter 4, attending to your food without the distraction of a phone or television is one way you can make eating more delightful. Whether you want to attune yourself to your meal or the people with whom you are sharing it, having a no-technology rule for mealtimes will help you eat more mindfully.

But removing the devices is only one part of the equation; you must also create new connection habits to replace your habits of regular checking and scrolling. A few years ago, I interviewed Brianne DeRosa of The Family Dinner Project on my podcast. The coauthor of *Eat, Laugh, Talk: The Family Dinner Playbook*, Brianne recommends intentionally creating fun and play at the dinner table to encourage connection, conversation, and laughter.

As you prepare your evening meal, think through a few questions that might get everyone talking. Use a conversation book, card deck, or internet search to fuel your creativity. Consider assigning this task to various members of your family. If you're eating alone, use the questions for your own inner contemplation.

Place a note on your table that says "question of the day." This will serve as a visual cue. Write out the questions or discussion topics so they're handy. You might also plan ahead with several questions prepped for the week. You will reap many rewards with this habit, including a deep connection with yourself and others, the ability to enjoy and savor your food, and feelings of gratitude.

Spread Love and Encouragement

People use social media for all sorts of reasons but mostly, as I see it, to share their joys and sorrows. It's a way of finding validation, belonging, and support. As I sift through people's posts and pictures, I may notice any number of feelings, including happiness and gratitude but also annoyance, judgment, and even envy.

If I'm mindful, I'll notice how people's posts make me feel, but I'll also notice how my interactions with what I see—my comments or likes—potentially impact how *other* people feel. A negative comment or my participation in a combative online debate is likely to sow seeds of discontent, in myself and in others, so I've made a commitment to using social media with the intention to actively spread love and encouragement.

As you log in to your chosen social media platform, set the intention to add and gain positivity. Deliberately focus on posts and pictures that make you feel good and actively avoid those that don't. When you see someone sharing some good news, leave an encouraging comment. You might even say aloud, "Yay you!" Conversely, when someone shares their challenges, feel and send compassion. Consider sending them a follow-up text or giving them a phone call.

As you use some of the habits in this chapter to reduce the amount of time spent mindlessly scrolling, begin to anchor this love and encouragement practice by taking a mindful pause before you pick up your device. Each time you engage in this habit, you will be rewarded with a feeling of goodwill and enthusiasm for others. You will also feel less pulled into negativity.

Use an Unplug Box

One of the reasons people may look at their smartphones so often is because they're usually somewhere in their sight line. It's common to place your devices conveniently within reach, but by doing so, they become a constant cue, especially if the notifications are turned on. To mindfully release the hold your phone has on you and to diminish the constant reminder to pick it up, check, and scroll, put it out of sight and out of mind.

To do this, you may need a new home base for your devices. Do a quick search for "unplug box" on Etsy, and you'll find dozens of crafty iterations of this idea for stowing devices away when it's time to focus on more important things.

You can purchase an unplug box or create one yourself. I think one with a lid is best, but the box itself is less important than the habit of using it. Place the box where you usually keep your phone, perhaps on the kitchen counter. When it's time to unplug, place the device inside and set it to Do Not Disturb mode so you won't hear it. Decide on a time later when you'll allow yourself to return calls or texts.

Design this habit to coincide with something you usually do around the time you want to unplug, such as coming home from work or starting to cook dinner. You will be rewarded by a sense of calm and independence that comes with being disconnected from your device. It will satisfy your need to spend quality time with the people you love.

Buffer Mindfully

According to the Pew Research Center, 42 percent of mobile phone use is to stave off boredom. These days, it's not uncommon to look around a doctor's waiting room or drive by kids at a bus stop and notice that *everyone* is on a phone. It's as though everyone has become utterly intolerant of boredom. We seem to have forgotten that boredom is good for us, that it's often inside monotony that we experience mini rests and gain new insights and ideas.

The habit of reaching for the phone the moment you have downtime is a deeply rooted, knee-jerk behavior for many smartphone users. As a result, there are few or no buffer moments, or little spaces of time between tasks, in your day-to-day life because they are immediately filled with mindless scrolling.

Start by creating a list of things you can do when you're between tasks or waiting. Could you close your eyes and take a few mindful breaths or do a quick body scan? Could you think about things you are grateful for or do the RAIN practice? Choose one and make this your new go-to practice whenever you find yourself reaching for your phone.

Consider new behaviors that you'd like to develop, such as the mindfulness practices in this book. Connect the opportunity to practice with your buffer time. Decide that when you have downtime, you'll use it to practice mindfulness instead of further habituating mindlessness. The benefits of healthy boundaries, feeling less auto-mated around technology, and feeling less compulsive and reflexive will help this habit stick.

Breaking Bad Habits

One of the reasons it's hard to change ingrained technology habits is that so many of them release dopamine, which is a neurotransmitter associated with good feelings. Behaviors that feel good trigger the brain's reward system, and before long, a habit, perhaps even an addiction, is formed.

We truly are addicted to our devices. In his book *Irresistible: The Rise of Addictive Technology and the Business of Keeping Us Hooked*, author Adam Alter shares that the inability to put down the smartphone occurs by design. Big tech knows just how to keep you scrolling and watching by employing tactics like loading another episode before the one you're watching is done or using algorithms that keep showing you photos similar to ones you've previously liked.

It's important to be aware that you've been set up to automatically interact with your devices. Like a casino with no visible exit signs or clocks, your devices are designed to lure you in further, deeper, and longer. Knowing that technology companies deliberately draw you in means that you must be just as deliberate in your attempts to draw yourself out. This requires the cultivation of healthy habits, like those earlier in this chapter, as well as breaking some bad habits that impair your awareness.

Doubling Up

According to research by Nielsen, Americans use a secondary digital device while watching television 45 percent of the time. Whether you're scrolling through social media or texting, the doubling up of screens is making us doubly mindless, and researchers fear the ability to concentrate on one thing at a time is becoming an endangered human skill.

If that's of concern to you, consider how many times you double up on your devices. Do you scroll while you stream? Do you text while on Zoom? Have you noticed how quickly your attention fades when you try to focus on just one thing? Perhaps it's time to address this doubling-up dilemma.

One of the perks of monotasking with tech (e.g., using one device at a time) is that you can more easily access your mindful self in relation to the device you're on. For example, instead of using commercial breaks to scroll through your phone, you can do a quick body scan. You might notice that what you're watching is making you stressed or perhaps that you're snacking unconsciously. Using one screen at a time increases your ability to be aware and to notice how what you're doing is impacting how you're feeling.

As you begin some screen time, via your television or computer, move other devices, such as phones or tablets, out of reach. Remember, out of sight equals out of mind. If you have to walk across the room to check a text or scroll through your social feed, you'll be less likely to do it.

Unlimited Screen Time

The subject of limiting screen time usually focuses on children. While it's true that 21st-century kids are spending too much time on screens, so are the grown-ups. Nearly half of American adults spend over 11 hours per day listening to, watching, reading, or generally interacting with media, according to Nielsen.

If you're spending half of your day in digital distraction, what aren't you doing? Going outside, connecting meaningfully to people you care about, and being physically active are a few things that come to my mind. Imagine at the end of your life if you added up all the hours you spent looking at a screen and you were able to trade some back in for more time with friends and family. Would you trade those screen hours in? With this perspective, you can see that you may be missing out on what makes life rich and meaningful when you spend too much time with your devices.

To get an accurate and thorough picture of how much time you're spending on screens, track your screen time for a week. Once you know your number, make a commitment to reduce it by at least 10 percent. Set clear "off times," such as the tech-free time blocks and device-free dinners described earlier in this chapter. Consider nontech hobbies you'd like to pursue, such as reading, walking, or learning an instrument. Schedule your nontech activities for times when you'd normally mindlessly scroll or stream so you can replace the bad habits with good ones.

Tracking Your Progress

It's tempting to think of habit-tracking like it's a score-card, but this is not its intent. You can learn a lot from this data and use it to guide your habits appropriately.

HABIT	M	T	W	TH	F	SAT	S

KEY TAKEAWAYS

- Devices have filled our lives with convenience and entertainment but also tremendous distraction.
- Much of technology is designed to be used mind-lessly. It's vital to learn how to protect your attention.
- Habits that create healthy boundaries related to tech-nology aid you in using your devices more mindfully.
- When you track your screen time and work to reduce it, you begin to make more space for other meaning-ful aspects of your life.

CHAPTER 9

Peacefully Letting Go

Life can get heavy. Whether you're looking back through decades of trials and tribulations or simply feeling the burden that everyday living can sometimes inflict, everyone has, at some point, traversed turbulent days, months, even years. The most important thing to remember is—and I can't say this enough—you can't always change what happens to you, but you can change how you respond to it. You can also change how long you hold on to it. In this chapter, we'll explore how you can use your awareness to let go of negative attachments and resentment while fortifying forgiveness, compassion, and freedom.

Mindful Letting Go

In the spring of 2007, Marc and I decided it was time to start our family, and so we "took the goalie out of the net" (as Canadians like to call it) and crossed our fingers it wouldn't take too long. Month after month passed and still no baby. Well-meaning friends gave the advice to simply "let go."

If you've ever wanted something badly, you'll know that "letting go" is much easier said than done. Knowing how attached I was to becoming pregnant and how frustrated I was feeling, my mom sent me an article that suggested that instead of letting go, we learn to put things down. This was a game-changer for me. Letting go felt like I was giving up, but putting down was about simply giving my clinging and relentless attachment a rest.

This is a chapter about how you can engage differently with your own individual attachments. Notice how you may want things to turn out and how you may want the people in your life to behave. Consider how often you interact with your circumstances through a lens of "should," as in it "should" be different or it "shouldn't" be this way. Attachment and resistance cause suffering. This doesn't mean that you will stop wanting things or stop trying; it means that you will form habits that create a healthy detachment so your emotions aren't so wrapped up in external circumstances or results. In essence, you will learn to surrender to life as is rather than live in conflict with it.

Building Healthier Habits

It takes wisdom, courage, and strength to let go. It also takes lots of practice. Building habits that increase your ability to gracefully surrender, forgive, and detach will counteract tendencies to cling to thoughts about what you want and what you don't want. It takes time to undo these well-worn tendencies.

Attachments can cause you to be overly hard on yourself, but you can learn to become more self-compassionate. "Shoulds" can cause unfair judgments of others, but you can learn through habits to have more empathy and patience. One way to do this is to build behaviors into your life that help you pause and see other perspectives. Practicing letting go helps you release thoughts about how things should be and surrender to how they actually are. In this state of peace, you can access your ability to be kind, calm, and maybe even easygoing.

The key is practice, and luckily you have loads of opportunities each day to engage differently with life's ups and downs. Either in the moment or as you reflect back later, you will learn to see how letting go and being less attached gives you the power to steady yourself whenever your attachments threaten to overwhelm you.

Take a Self-Compassion Break

The world would be a much different place if everyone learned to be kinder to themselves. Maybe at some point in human history, it served us to push ourselves beyond our limits, but there's no use for this trait in modern times. Each person is doing the best they can each day with the knowledge and experience they've collected so far. There will be mistakes. There will be tough times. Let's cut ourselves some slack.

In Kristin Neff's book *Self-Compassion: The Proven Power of Being Kind to Yourself*, she writes that people are often reluctant to offer themselves self-compassion because they worry that being kinder to themselves will make them weak or lazy. But the truth is that through gentleness we build our resilience.

Sitting quietly, place a gentle hand on your heart or softly hold your own hands. Tune in to thoughts or circumstances that are troubling you or a recent moment when you were really hard on yourself. Maybe you sent an email with a typo, forgot something important, or let someone down. Take a moment to acknowledge that you wish it had gone differently. Label your anger, frustration, or disappointment. Now bring some tenderness to those feelings, like you would for a dear friend. Silently speak some encouraging words to yourself, such as "It's okay. People make mistakes." Soften your heart toward yourself.

Give yourself a self-compassion break at least once a day. Stack this habit with your nighttime routine so you're showing yourself this kindness right before falling asleep. The reward for this habit is the return to a sense of friendship and solidarity with yourself as you cultivate kindness and warmth.

Notice Similarities Instead of Differences

When you make a habit of setting aside ideological attachments and looking beyond interpersonal differences, you may be surprised to discover the similarities you share with people different from yourself. Most people, at their core, share a number of deep human values, like the wish to be safe, happy, and loved. When you can put yourself in another person's circumstances, you begin to see that, most of the time, the person is doing the best they can. By reframing your perspective to incorporate more patience, understanding, and compassion, you make more space and grace for others' missteps. It doesn't mean that you let people walk all over you; it means that once you set boundaries, you let things go for *your own* sake, or for your own sense of peace.

The next time someone does something that bothers you, take a moment to consider how you might react if you were in the same circumstances or saw things from their point of view. Contemplate ways you are similar to the person rather than judging your differences. Notice your common humanity, and send some compassion for their situation, even if it negatively impacts yours.

Practice this habit when you are waiting in line. As you look around, notice any judgments that pop into your mind; then try to replace them with commonalities you might notice. When you greet these thoughts with compassion, you will be rewarded with feelings of ease, peace, warmth, and kindness toward others and yourself.

Allow What Is

True surrender comes from acknowledging life as is. As events unfold around you, you have a choice to resist or accept them. But in terms of the event itself, it is what it is. Thinking otherwise is simply, as Buddhist meditation teacher Sharon Salzberg says, picking a fight with reality.

There is great peace in mindfully allowing things to be just as they are in this moment. This morning as I walked with my friend Smruti, rain began to pour down on us, and we had to end our walk early. That circumstance could have been met with frustration or disappointment, but that wouldn't have changed the rain. Rather than shaking our fists at the sky, we directed our energy toward locating a dry spot to chat.

Take a quiet moment in your day to reflect on a circumstance that you wish was different. It could be something as simple as disappointment in food you'd ordered or frustration that a client was late for a meeting. Notice any agitation and, as you breathe, soften around this feeling. Repeat a phrase such as "it is what it is" as you imagine the agitation leaving your body on the exhale. Continue to bring a spirit of acceptance as you slowly let the circumstance go.

Stack this habit with the habit of a daily walk or quiet commute. As your tension melts and you begin to feel at peace, your brain will feel rewarded, and the habit will come with increasing ease.

Look for the Roses amid the Thorns

One of the best ways to let go when you're faced with difficulties or frustrations is to explore how a circumstance could be happening *for* you rather than *to* you. This means you look for another perspective, one where a troubling circumstance may have some hidden benefit. Maybe not getting the job means better doors are about to open. Perhaps canceled plans will give you a chance to catch up on things at home. The idea is that in all things there are two sides to the coin, and you sometimes need to intentionally choose to look at the good side to prevent fixating on the bad.

When you practice looking for roses amid the thorns, you learn to find the beauty in difficult circumstances and allow them to be opportunities for growth or learning rather than things that drag you down.

Begin by calling to mind a situation you wish had gone differently. Consider the thorny aspects, such as how it made you feel or the fallout it caused. Bring some compassion to yourself and the others involved. Now, consider something good that came from the situation or good that will come down the road. Think about what the situation taught you or how you had to rise to meet it. Consider how it may have given you the opportunity to practice something you're working on, such as being kinder to yourself or others.

Practice this habit during mealtimes, perhaps as part of dinner discussion. The habit will be reinforced by your feeling of connection with others and the ability to be at peace when faced with life's ups and downs.

Accept Impermanence

Life is impermanent, fluid, and in constant flux. Painful experiences, along with joyful moments, are temporary. Nothing lasts forever. Such is the nature of life.

Impermanence is an essential facet of our existence. We are each born as infants but then dramatically grow and change in the months and years that follow. In fact, the body completely remakes itself at a cellular level every 7 to 10 years. Moreover, the seasons change every few months, the weather changes minute by minute, and the planet changes position every microsecond.

There's value in acknowledging that life exists in a state of flux. Embracing the impermanent nature of living allows you to apply a softer grip on your existence, which helps you relate to your circumstances with more peace and perspective.

Think of a situation in your life that is currently causing you stress or concern. When did the situation begin? Now, think of a troubling situation that has passed. Consider how your circumstances, even the good ones, are always impermanent. Look around your environment and notice the things that are always changing: the time, houseplants, your children, or the angle of the sunlight coming through the window. Breathe into the process of loosening your grip on how things should or shouldn't be. Try mentally repeating the phrase "This too shall pass."

When you have a stressful moment, use this practice as an opportunity to notice that all things pass eventually. Your reward is the understanding that this too shall pass and the strength and self-confidence that are the natural by-products of your resilience.

Breaking Bad Habits

Negativity is toxic. When you continually revisit your resentments and hurts, you allow your stress response to restart over and over. The body tenses up and releases cortisol, the breath becomes shallower, and the heart beats faster. All of this can happen as the result of a single thought, perhaps about something that may have happened months, maybe years, ago.

When you make a regular date with negativity, it becomes a habit. It gets wired into your mind, guides your tendencies, and perhaps even settles into your identity. Thankfully, the brain can be rewired. You can change how you respond to life, and when you do this enough times, you can transform not only your responses to the world around you but who you are on a deeper level.

Harboring negativity and being a martyr are ways of holding on to negative circumstances and experiences rather than peacefully and gently letting them go.

Buddhist teachers often tell the story of the two arrows. The first is shot at you from outside your life. It represents something that happens to you. But the second comes from your own hands and represents the pain and suffering you inflict on yourself when you hold on to what has happened to you. As you break the two habits that follow, you'll learn to put down that second arrow.

Harboring Negativity

In 2019, my family and I traveled to France for our summer vacation. The first few days were wonderful, until thieves broke into our car at a rest stop outside Paris, taking with them Marc's computer, our tablet, and our passports. For the rest of the day, we filled out police reports and worked out how and where we would get our passports replaced. But the next morning, we made a conscious decision as a family to simply let it go. We didn't share the experience with anyone back home, didn't post about it on social media, and barely talked about it again for the rest of our trip. It was done, over. There was no need to cast a dark cloud over our trip by constantly bemoaning something we couldn't change.

When you hang on to negativity, it continues to flavor your days with more negativity. When you continue to rehash your resentments in your mind or with others, you keep sipping poison from your own cup. Forgiveness and letting go might seem like noble acts to do for other people, but in reality, they are gifts you give yourself.

The next time you find yourself rehashing a negative experience in your mind or telling the story to another person, use it as an opportunity to practice looking for roses amid the thorns (see page 117). Notice that you're telling the story again, but finish it with a different ending, one where you learned or grew as a result.

Playing the Martyr

During tough times, it can be helpful to share your woes with a close confidant. It can be hard to suffer in silence, and it can be reassuring to be able to lean on someone to help you talk through a difficult circumstance. But there does comes a time when the telling and retelling of your difficulties start to become a martyr complex that threatens to become a part of who you are.

While some may believe in the virtue of suffering, I believe in the virtue of transcending. Everyone is going to face difficulties at one time or another. Some may knock you down for a bit, but each difficulty offers a chance to rise above the events rather than dragging the heavy weight of your cumulative adversities like luggage. In some cases, though not all, the best thing you can do after you've worked out your hurts and hardships is to bravely move on.

This does not mean that you bypass healing or stuff things down. A good friend or therapist can be a real ally in your journey through difficult times, emotions, and memories. But your future can only be defined by your past if you define yourself as a victim instead of a victor.

Think of an adversity story you've been carrying or telling for a long time. Have you found the roses, or do you still fixate on the thorns? What could this situation teach you about boundaries or self-care? Consider what you could learn from it and how you could grow, and then make a commitment to move on.

Tracking Your Progress

If you see benefit in tracking your habits, support this practice by making it easy, visible, and convenient. See how you can integrate habit-tracking as a standard practice in your day.

HABIT	M	T	W	TH	F	SAT	S

KEY TAKEAWAYS

- You can learn to relate differently to your attachments by creating a healthy detachment so that your inner state isn't wrapped up in external circumstances.
- You can learn to surrender to life as is rather than live in conflict with it.
- Harboring negativity and being a martyr can cause you to cling to negative experiences rather than peacefully and gently letting them go.
- When you habituate mindfulness practices, you can cultivate more peace, compassion, and resilience.

CHAPTER 10

Mindful on the Move

I see so many opportunities to practice mindfulness beyond formal meditation and so many places in the day that can be used to create the habit of being fully present in the moment. Cultivating mindfulness is less about doing something new and more about bringing presence to what you're already doing. When you bring yourself fully into the present moment, even when you're thrown into the monotony of laundry or waiting at the post office, you can experience the moment in ways that spark gratitude, happiness, and even joy. In this chapter, you'll learn how to integrate mindful moments into everyday living.

Mindful Journey

In between work and play is just plain ol' living: errands, commutes, taking the dog to the vet, dropping the kids off at soccer, mailing a package, picking up a prescription, hitting a drive-through for a coffee–you get the idea.

While it might be tempting to think that the "good life" is one in which you no longer have to do life's menial tasks, the truth is that peace and happiness come from having a joyful approach, not from eliminating all of our impositions. My friend Angie B. regularly asks, "How can I find pleasure in this moment?" It's as though she is continuously scanning her environment for delight. And it shows; she is the most vivacious person I know.

I think of my morning meditation practice as my anchor for the day. Once I settle into the formal ritual of tapping into my mindful self, it becomes the north star I orient myself toward until bedtime. From then on, I'm simply practicing what I was doing on my cushion: guiding my attention back to the present moment. Of course, I often lose myself and slip into automated mode just like everyone else. But with my mindfulness habits, like those you'll discover in this chapter, I set little portals to mindfulness along my path each day, and opening each one helps bring me back to myself and to the now.

Building Healthier Habits

Building healthy habits rests on a few basic pillars: when you repeat behaviors consistently, they become habits, and when habits feel good, they stick. In her book *Good Habits, Bad Habits*, Wendy Wood considers the influence of a third pillar: context. In her research, Wood discovered that context, or environment, heavily influences behavior. This is why many habits are done not only at the same time every day but in the same place. Environment is a powerful behavioral prompt.

Since most of us typically do many of the same things every day and move around and through the same places each week, using environment to prompt behavior isn't too difficult. For example, I can anchor a habit with getting into my car, standing in a line, or walking down my street, since these are things that I already do habitually.

When you realize how much influence your surroundings have on your habits, you will see that context can propel your behavior. The mindful on-the-go habits you'll find in this chapter leverage the power of context to support you in creating more mindful states. Using your environment as a trigger for your behavior allows the habits to adhere to a physical place and become more rooted.

Be Mindful about Money

Money has grown from simply being a tool for commerce to becoming a way to measure worth and importance. Most of us agree that real value comes from who we are on the inside, regardless of how much money we have. We know that money doesn't make us good or better people and that there is a limit to how much happiness it can bring.

Yet there is an energy to money. It moves through our hands and bank accounts, and it occupies our thoughts and provokes anxiety. When you tune in to your energy around money, you will likely notice that you have strong thoughts and feelings about it. Those thoughts and feelings are the foundation of your relationship with money. As Lynne Twist shares in her book *The Soul of Money*, it is your interpretation of money and the meaning you attach to it that give it so much power.

Each time you interact with money, you have an opportunity to examine your relationship to it and how it makes you feel. Notice how you respond physically and emotionally when you spend it, move it, or give it. Consider and examine your beliefs about money. This practice is a research expedition, meant to increase your awareness of the influence money has on your life.

Anchor this practice to a specific money-related activity you do regularly, such as shopping, banking, or reconciling your budget. The rewards that will help you reinforce this habit are a new and healthy awareness of the role money plays in your life and an increased sense of gratitude and calm.

Create Space for Silence

As I head out on my morning or evening walk, I often see others in my subdivision out for a stroll as well, many with their phones in hand and wearing earbuds. It wasn't that long ago that I, too, used my walk to catch up on podcasts and audiobooks. It felt like a two-for-one, allowing me to do two things I loved at once. But there came a time when my schedule shifted and I had less time in the morning for my meditation practice, so I decided to use my walk as a stand-in for my seated practice. Off I went, leaving my phone at home. Words can't even begin to describe how satisfying it was to be outside with my awareness focused on the world around me instead of the sounds in my ears. It was as though I was seeing my neighborhood with fresh eyes.

Notice all the moments in your day when you add chatter and background noise to your life via the radio, podcasts, or audiobooks. Pick one or two instances, perhaps during your workout, walk, or commute, to mindfully and intentionally have silence. As you move or travel, narrow your attention to your senses: What do you hear, see, smell, and feel? Listen to the birds, notice your surroundings, be on the lookout for beauty. Slow your pace so you can soak up what's happening around you rather than be focused on where you're going.

Have this be something you do alongside a morning or evening routine. Perhaps it becomes your new evening commute after you finish your workday at home or as a nice break during your workday. The quiet you experience when you engage in this habit rewards you with a reconnection to yourself. As you absorb the moment, feel your feelings, and notice your thoughts, you get to know yourself—and the world around you—better.

Put Your Phone in the Back Seat

Distracted driving is a major safety concern. It's astonishing to see how many drivers have the steering wheel in one hand and their smartphone in the other, even as they're speeding down the highway. The National Safety

Council reports that cell phone use while driving leads to 1.6 million crashes each year.

Knowing how incredibly addictive phones are, the best remedy is to keep them out of reach and out of sight. By creating friction (making the behavior more difficult), you weaken the hold an existing habit has on you.

When you first get into your car and shut the door, take a moment to complete any back-and-forth text exchanges you might currently be engaged in. Let the person know you're about to start driving. Then place the phone in the back seat out of sight and out of reach. Give yourself a mental high five or fist pump for taking such a healthy step.

Create a new routine for when you first get into your car. Use the clicking of your seat belt as a cue to place your phone in the back seat. As an added measure, set your phone settings to lock when driving. The rewards for this habit are as practical as they are healthy and mindful. By decreasing compulsive behavior related to your phone, you will enjoy a feeling of independence and self-confidence while also being safer on the road.

Practice Street Loving-Kindness

A few years ago, I listened to an interview with Sharon Salzberg, cofounder of the Insight Meditation Society and author of several books on mindfulness. In the interview, she shared that she often practices Metta meditation (also known as loving-kindness) as she walks down the street, silently wishing that the people she encounters feel safe, happy, and free from suffering. She laughed and called it "guerilla loving-kindness," a sort of ambush of compassion and care. Of course, no one she encounters has any idea what she's thinking, but the practice expands her own heart and how interconnected she feels with others.

This is such a simple but profound way to find presence within the common humanity we all share. When I wish others well, especially strangers and those who are different from me, I expand my circle of compassion to include more than my loved ones or people who are just like me.

The next time you find yourself walking down a busy street or through a busy space, use it as an opportunity to send well-wishes to others. As you look at those around you, silently repeat these phrases: *May you be well. May you be happy. May you be free from suffering.* When you're done, perhaps give yourself the same loving-kindness offering.

Pick a route you walk often and make this the environment that you practice this habit in. See how wide your circle of loving-kindness becomes. The warmth and empathy toward others created by this habit will also make you feel good, which will reinforce the habit. A sense of common humanity and connectedness also offers a sense of belonging.

Wait Gratefully

When you think about it, you likely spend a lot of your life waiting. This week alone I waited in line at the grocery store, I waited for my kung fu class to begin, I waited for my daughter as she had her archery lesson, and I waited on hold with an airline. Often, waiting feels tedious. You may reach for your phone for immediate relief. But what if you could trade your propensity for distraction for a moment of gratitude instead? Instead of feeling frustrated or impatient or mindlessly ruminating or scrolling, use your waiting moments to actively and deliberately cultivate more gratitude in your life.

The next time you find yourself waiting, make a list of 5 to 10 things you're grateful for, finding people or things in your environment to appreciate. For example, you may be grateful for the kind staff and the immense selection in your local grocery store. You may be grateful for the beautiful setting and the chance to be outside as you wait for your child to finish soccer practice. Make the commitment: *When I am waiting, I will look around me and practice gratitude.*

Practice this habit in one particular place you find yourself waiting in each week. Consider keeping a gratitude journal or notebook in your car, backpack, or bag. The reward for this habit is feeling like you've made good use of your time rather than mindlessly scrolling. It can also heighten positive feelings of connection and appreciation and instill a sense of purpose—all of which will help with habit formation.

Breaking Bad Habits

It's easy to default to the automated mind when you're on the go. Day-to-day comings and goings don't require much focus or effort, and for the most part, you can simply go through the motions. The more often you do something, the more likely you are to sleepwalk through it. But if your aim is to live more mindfully, it's vital that you punctuate your day with thresholds of awareness, with little invitations to return to the present moment. Even when you are busy, you can build harbors of stillness and retreat, which help break the tendency to be in constant motion and relentlessly purposeful.

When I am in go mode, I can be like a whirling dervish. Once I get started, it's as though momentum carries me onward, and I just don't stop. This mode feels compulsive, even hypnotic. The only way to halt its hold on me is to hit the brake and stop. The bad habits covered ahead—a lack of solitude and constant busyness—are like accelerators for your life. The antidote I suggest for each of them will help you decelerate.

Lack of Solitude

Modern life simply isn't oriented toward solitude. In fact, many people have developed quite an aversion to being quietly alone with themselves, as one University of Virginia study found. Researchers gave subjects the option to either do nothing and spend time with their thoughts or receive an electric shock. A quarter of the women and two-thirds of the men chose the shock.

Having established a morning practice of alone time, I've learned to love solitude, even crave it. But I wasn't always this way. Until I created the habit and the familiarity of being quietly alone with myself, I spent my entire day accompanied by a computer, a phone, a television, a radio, and other people. Alone felt uncomfortable, even agitating.

According to Mihaly Csikszentmihalyi, author of *Flow*, we spend about one-third of our waking hours alone. However, there's a common tendency to turn all of those hours over to distraction, entertainment, and task completion. A mindful life needs solitude. When you establish a habit of daily solitude while also looking for moments to embrace being alone with yourself, you begin to not only build your tolerance of stillness but also love the restorative gifts solitude offers.

Create blocks of time for solitude. These blocks may already exist in your week, but you currently fill them with digital distraction or chatter. Practice being alone, with nothing to distract you, once each day for 10 minutes. Go for a stroll, sit quietly, turn the radio off while driving. Just be.

Always Being Busy

For those of us who find ourselves needing to be constantly productive, being busy can start to feel like a default mode. For some, leisure equals laziness. That's unfortunate because it is through rest that recalibration, reorientation, and refueling occur.

In his book *Sabbath: Finding Rest, Renewal, and Delight in Our Busy Lives*, author Wayne Muller makes a case for intentionally and deliberately setting aside downtime. Much like a field must be allowed to be dormant between growing seasons, so too should we allow ourselves to be unproductive and idle.

Isn't this what the weekend was designed for? Sadly, weekends without rest can leave you feeling both forlorn for what didn't get done—including rest—and anxiety-ridden as you face the onslaught of activity looming ahead in the impending workweek. It doesn't have to be this way.

My family began the ritual of a weekly unplug day a few years ago, and the impact has been extraordinary. On Sunday, we stay home and just chill out. We feast, we nap, we loaf and laze. Sound delightful? Try it out yourself. Start clearing your calendar every Sunday (or Saturday), and let others know you'll be unavailable. Do a puzzle, go for a walk, read a book, watch a movie, take a bath, bake a cake, play a game. Take back one day of your week and make it just for rest and play.

Tracking Your Progress

Habit-tracking allows you to see if a habit is working. Your discoveries are not a reflection of who you are or how disciplined you are; they are a reflection of how well the habit is built. If a habit isn't sticking, it's not because you're lazy or lack willpower. It's likely because you used the wrong anchor or pairing, started too big, or weren't specific enough about the behavior.

HABIT	M	T	W	TH	F	SAT	S

KEY TAKEAWAYS

- Cultivating mindfulness is less about doing new things and more about doing what you're already doing with more presence.
- The minutiae of life account for many of your waking hours each week, and they provide innumerable opportunities to practice mindfulness.
- Environment is a powerful behavioral prompt. Use the places you're in regularly to anchor healthy habits.
- A lack of solitude and an endless need to be busy accelerate the pace of life, which makes being present challenging.

RESOURCES

Mindfulness and Meditation

Brach, Tara. *True Refuge: Finding Peace and Freedom in Your Own Awakened Heart*. New York: Bantam Books, 2012.

Chödrön, Pema. *How to Meditate: A Practical Guide to Making Friends with Your Mind*. Boulder, CO: Sounds True, Inc., 2013.

Dukes, Timothy. *The Present Parent Handbook: 26 Simple Tools to Discover That This Moment, This Action, This Thought, This Feeling Is Exactly Why I Am Here*. Sanger, CA: Familius, 2017.

Dyer, Wayne W. *Getting in the Gap: Making Conscious Contact with God Through Meditation*. Carlsbad, CA: Hay House, Inc., 2003.

Kabat-Zinn, Jon. *Falling Awake: How to Practice Mindfulness in Everyday Life*. New York: Hachette Books, 2018.

Smalley, Susan L., and Diana Winston. *Fully Present: The Science, Art, and Practice of Mindfulness*. Boston: Da Capo Press, 2010.

Watkins, Light. *Bliss More: How to Succeed in Meditation Without Really Trying*. New York: Ballantine Books, 2018.

Books about Creating Habits

Clear, James. *Atomic Habits: An Easy and Proven Way to Build Good Habits and Break Bad Ones*. New York: Avery, 2018.

Duhigg, Charles. *The Power of Habit: Why We Do What We Do in Life and Business*. New York: Random House, 2012.

Fogg, BJ. *Tiny Habits: The Small Changes That Change Everything*. New York: Houghton Mifflin Harcourt, 2020.

Goldsmith, Marshall, and Mark Reiter. *Triggers: Creating Behavior That Lasts–Becoming the Person You Want to Be*. New York: Crown Business, 2015.

Rubin, Gretchen. *Better Than Before: What I Learned About Making and Breaking Habits–To Sleep More, Quit Sugar, Procrastinate Less, and Generally Build a Happier Life*. New York: Broadway Books, 2015.

Wood, Wendy. *Good Habits, Bad Habits: The Science of Making Positive Changes That Stick*. New York: Farrar, Straus and Giroux, 2019.

More of My Favorite Books

Beavan, Colin. *How to Be Alive: A Guide to the Kind of Happiness That Helps the World*. New York: Dey Street Books, 2017.

Carver, Courtney. *Soulful Simplicity: How Living with Less Can Lead to So Much More*. New York: TarcherPerigee, 2017.

Dweck, Carol S. *Mindset: The New Psychology of Success*. New York: Ballantine Books, 2016.

Foer, Joshua. *Moonwalking with Einstein: The Art and Science of Remembering Everything*. New York: Penguin Group, 2011.

McGonigal, Kelly. *The Willpower Instinct: How Self-Control Works, Why It Matters, and What You Can Do to Get More of It*. New York: Avery, 2013.

McKeown, Greg. *Essentialism: The Disciplined Pursuit of Less*. New York: Crown Business, 2014.

Muller, Wayne. *Sabbath: Finding Rest, Renewal, and Delight in Our Busy Lives*. New York: Bantam, 1999.

Singer, Michael A. *The Untethered Soul: The Journey Beyond Yourself*. Oakland, CA: New Harbinger Publications, Inc., 2007.

REFERENCES

Alter, Adam. *Irresistible: The Rise of Addictive Technology and the Business of Keeping Us Hooked.* New York: Penguin Press, 2017.

American Psychological Association. "Give Me a Break." Accessed January 2021. APA.org/monitor/2019/01/break.

Babauta, Leo. "Death Isn't the End." Zen Habits. Accessed January 2021. zenhabits.net.

Babb, Michelle. *Mastering Mindful Eating.* Seattle: Sasquatch Books, 2020.

Bisbort, Alan. "The Shocking Truth." *University of Virginia Magazine.* February 24, 2015. UVAMagazine.org/articles/the_shocking_truth.

Brown, Stuart. *Play: How It Shapes the Brain, Opens the Imagination, and Invigorates the Soul.* New York: Avery, 2009.

Buettner, Dan. "The Secrets of Long Life." *National Geographic.* November 2005. BlueZones.com/wp-content/uploads/2015/01/Nat_Geo_LongevityF.pdf.

Cameron, Julia. *The Artist's Way.* New York: J. P. Tarcher/Putnam, 2002.

Carver, Courtney. *Soulful Simplicity: How Living with Less Can Lead to So Much More.* New York: TarcherPerigee, 2017.

Cision. "National Safety Council Estimates That at Least 1.6 Million Crashes Are Caused Each Year by Drivers Using Cell Phones and Texting." January 12, 2010. PRNewsWire.com/news-releases/national-safety-council-estimates-that-at-least-16-million-crashes-are-caused-each-year-by-drivers-using-cell-phones-and-texting-81252807.html.

Csikszentmihalyi, Mihaly. *Flow*. New York: Harper & Row, 1990.

DeRosa, Brianne. *Eat, Laugh, Talk: The Family Dinner Playbook*. Sanger, CA: Familius, 2019.

Dietz, Andrew. *Follow the Meander: An Indirect Route to a More Creative Life*. Atlanta, GA: Silent Thunder Press, 2020.

Fogg, BJ. *Tiny Habits: The Small Changes That Change Everything*. New York: Houghton Mifflin Harcourt, 2020.

Friedman, Howard S., and Leslie R. Martin. *The Longevity Project*. New York: Hudson Street Press, 2011.

Gervis, Zoya. "America's Lunch Break Is Fading Away, Study Finds." *SWNS Digital*. August 30, 2018. SWNSdigital.com/2018/08 /americas-lunch-break-is-fading-away-study-finds.

Goyal, Madhav, Sonal Singh, Erica M. S. Sibinga, Neda F. Gould, Anastasia Rowland-Seymour, Ritu Sharma, Zackary Berger, et al. "Meditation Programs for Psychological Stress and Well-Being: A Systematic Review and Meta-Analysis." *JAMA Internal Medicine* 3, no. 174 (2014): 357–68. doi:10.1001/jamainternmed.2013.13018.

Greater Good Magazine. "What Is Mindfulness?" Accessed April 1, 2021. GreaterGood.Berkeley.edu/topic/mindfulness/definition.

Hanh, Thich Nhat. *The Miracle of Mindfulness*. Boston: Beacon Press, 1976.

Harvard Health Publishing. "Giving Thanks Can Make You Happier." November 2011. Health.Harvard.edu/healthbeat/giving-thanks-can-make -you-happier.

Jacobs, A. J. *Thanks A Thousand*. New York: TEDBooks, 2018.

Kho, Nancy Davis. *Thank-You Project: Cultivating Happiness One Letter of Gratitude at a Time.* New York: Running Press, 2019.

Kuile, Casper ter. *The Power of Ritual: Turning Everyday Activities into Soulful Practices.* New York: HarperCollins, 2020.

Levine, James. *Get Up!: Why Your Chair Is Killing You and What You Can Do About It.* London: St. Martin's Publishing Group, 2014.

Lisitsa, Ellie. "The Four Horseman: Contempt." The Gottman Institute. May 13, 2013. Gottman.com/blog/the-four-horsemen-contempt.

Manieri, Kristen. "The Family Dinner Project with Brianne De Rosa." *Kristen Manieri Podcast.* KristenManieri.com/2019/11/12 /the-family-dinner-project.

Muller, Wayne. *Sabbath: Finding Rest, Renewal, and Delight in Our Busy Lives.* New York: Bantam, 1999.

Neff, Kristin. *Self-Compassion: The Proven Power of Being Kind to Yourself.* New York: William Morrow, 2011.

Nielsen. "Juggling Act: Audiences Have More Media at Their Disposal and Are Using Them Simultaneously." December 12, 2018. Nielsen.com /us/en/insights/article/2018/juggling-act-audiences-have -more-media-at-their-disposal-and-are-using-them-simultaneously.

Nielsen. "Time Flies: U.S. Adults Now Spend Nearly Half a Day Interacting with Media." July 31, 2018. Nielsen.com/us/en/insights/article /2018/time-flies-us-adults-now-spend-nearly-half-a-day -interacting-with-media.

Organisation for Economic Co-operation and Development. "Balancing Paid Work, Unpaid Work and Leisure." May 3, 2018. OECD.org /gender/balancing-paid-work-unpaid-work-and-leisure.htm.

Owen, Erika. *The Art of Flaneuring: How to Wander with Intention and Discover a Better Life.* New York: Simon & Schuster, Inc., 2019.

Pillay, Srini. *Tinker Dabble Doodle Try: Unlock the Power of the Unfocused Mind.* New York: Ballantine Books, 2017.

Price, Catherine. *How to Break Up with Your Phone: The 30-Day Plan to Take Back Your Life.* New York: Ten Speed Press, 2018.

Smith, Aaron. "Americans and Their Cell Phones." Pew Research Center. August 15, 2011. PewResearch.org/internet/2011/08/15/americans -and-their-cell-phones.

Thorne, Blake. "How Distractions at Work Take Up More Time Than You Think." *I Done This.* February 13, 2020. Blog.IDoneThis.com /distractions-at-work.

Tolle, Eckhart. *The Power of Now.* Novato, CA: New World Library, 1999.

Twist, Lynne. *The Soul of Money.* New York: W. W. Norton & Company, Inc., 2003.

Wood, Wendy. *Good Habits, Bad Habits: The Science of Making Positive Changes That Stick.* New York: Farrar, Straus and Giroux, 2019.

Younger, Rebekah. *Be, Awake, Create.* Oakland, CA: Reveal Press, 2019.

INDEX

Acknowledgments

Marc, thank you for being a constant source of support, encouragement, and love.

I'm immensely grateful to Elizabeth and Aly, who not only tolerate my constant chatter about habits but also have (seemingly) embraced my zealot-like passion for my work.

I have great gratitude for Joe Cho, for believing I was the best person for this endeavor, and to Kayla Park and Erika Sloan, who edited this book with thoughtful care and precision.

But I also have my mom to thank for giving early drafts of this book her eagle eyes and for showering me with praise. Mom, thank you for being my cheerleader.

About the Author

 **Kristen Manieri** is a certified habits coach as well as a certified mindfulness teacher through the International Mindfulness Teachers Association (IMTA). Kristen is the host of the *60 Mindful Minutes* podcast, which launched in 2017 and has produced inspiring and thought-provoking interviews with over 130 authors. Kristen holds a BA in English literature and communication studies. She shares her life with her two daughters, her husband, and their three cats. Connect with her at KristenManieri.com or on Instagram @kristenmanieri_.

CPSIA information can be obtained
at www.ICGtesting.com
Printed in the USA
LVHW072055240521
688355LV00011B/58